KU-545-845

PLANTING THE PERFECT GARDEN

PLANTING
THE
PERFECT GARDEN

*Beautiful designs for pots, borders,
town and country gardens*

David Stuart

MACMILLAN
LONDON

Acknowledgements

So many gardeners and their gardens have helped in the making of this book that it is difficult to thank them all. However, I am especially grateful to the garden owners who let me see and photograph their gardens, and were then kind enough to help with the plant identifications once I decided which gardens to use (itself a difficult task as so many were lovely).

I should also like to thank the many other garden owners who were kind enough to let me look at their gardens, but to which either the day or my photographs failed to do justice.

Thanks are also due to the National Trust for England and Wales for permissions to use photographs of the fine gardens in their care, and especially the head gardener at Powys Castle for much help naming plants in the sumptuous borders he has created there.

There are a number of garden owners I must also thank for their kind hospitality, especially Mrs Fuller of Crossing House, a garden crammed to bursting with good plants, Mr Alan Roger of Dundonnel, Mrs Mary McMurtrie of Balbithan and Mr Francis Egerton.

Lastly, with a book so heavily based on lists, I should like to thank the editorial staff at Macmillan, whose patience and eye for detail made up for my own deficiencies in such matters.

Copyright © David Stuart 1991

Design and drawings by Louise Millar
and Tom Emlyn Williams

All rights reserved. No reproduction, copy or transmission of this publication may be made without written permission. No paragraph of this publication may be reproduced, copied or transmitted save with written permission or in accordance with the provisions of the Copyright Act 1956 (as amended). Any person who does any unauthorised act in relation to this publication may be liable to criminal prosecution and civil claims for damages.

First published 1991 by
MACMILLAN LONDON LIMITED
Cavaye Place London SW10 9PG
and Basingstoke

Associated companies in Auckland, Delhi, Dublin, Gaborone, Hamburg, Harare, Hong Kong, Johannesburg, Kuala Lumpur, Lagos, Manzini, Melbourne, Mexico City, Nairobi, New York, Singapore and Tokyo

ISBN 0–333–45668–8

A CIP catalogue record for this book is available from the British Library

Typeset by Macmillan Production Limited

Printed in Hong Kong

Contents

Introduction

The idea for this book grew out of frustration at the lack of information about the plantings shown in many modern garden books. Although they are often crammed with wonderful photographs, they give only brief captions so that, while the central group of plants might be identified, there is often no information on the lovely things growing behind or to one side of it. However marvellous the image given by the picture, there is no way that the reader, especially if new to gardening, can recreate the planting in his or her own garden. The photographs in this book are of plantings in which almost all the plants are identified, so if you find a photograph you like, it will be easy for you to recreate the planting for yourself. Nearly all the plants are easily obtainable and easily grown and there are also suggestions for adapting the planting (if necessary) to your own site and requirements.

As with all beauty, perfection in the garden is in the eye of the beholder. Some gardeners adore the most florid begonias, while others like rock plants so small you almost need a magnifying lens to see them. You will not find any begonias in this book, nor much traditionally associated with rockeries. Instead, I have tried to capture a rather specific style of gardening, among the number that are current, and one which I find irresistible. It is green and romantic, even rather untidy, not given to loud colours or violent clashes of colour, and the emphasis is as much on interesting foliage and foliage combinations as it is on the colour of flowers. It also makes use of the humble and well-known garden flora, though often handled in clever ways.

While many of the gardens shown do contain rare plants, the illustrations included here are of parts of the planting filled mainly with plants that are easy to obtain and grow – there is almost nothing here that will need expert gardening.

Most of the plantings represent a synthesis of the planting styles that have been evolving in fashionable gardens over the last hundred years or so, once the malevolent influence of the Victorian bedding movement (with its sheets of scarlet verbena, yellow calceolaria and blue lobelia) lost its power. Here, old-fashioned plants, as well as new ones, combine to make luscious herbaceous borders like the one in Aberdeenshire on page 84 and borders with the subtlest of colour schemes, potagers and parterres, woodland gardens, patio and terrace gardens, and gardens of cottages and manor houses.

All the gardens shown have been explored for ways of putting plants together that look especially good. Although these gardens are all the result of vast labours, this book shows you how to put some lovely plantings together in a weekend or two (though you will have to wait for two seasons at least before they mature), and suggests ways, if you have only a little room, to make the plantings look good for as long a season as possible, either by adding other kinds of plants, or by substituting a few different plants for some of the basic scheme.

The gardens shown have usually been created by passionately keen gardeners, many of whom garden every day. Any maintenance problems are discussed – some of the 'wild' plantings are especially deceptive – and I've suggested simplifications that a busy owner might carry out without losing the charm of the scene. I have also tried to include a wide range of types of plantings, from those suitable for a biggish tub or a border in a tiny shaded patio, to those for formal pools, ponds, grand herbaceous borders and complicated cottage-garden tangles. Consequently, your own patch, whatever its size, shape or location, can soon look as enchanting as the gardens shown here.

Of course, photographs are never quite enough; they show a garden at a moment of one day, in only part of the season. One of the fascinations of gardening is the way things are constantly changing, so a photograph can give only the briefest guide to the pleasures in store. If you need further inspiration for your planning, visit as many gardens as you can. Hundreds of interesting gardens are open for Garden Scheme days, though the quality can be quite variable, and even the demonstration gardens of colleges of horticulture might be worth a visit (although you will also see acres of concrete 'features', plastic hanging baskets and bedding plants). If you don't have time for such exploration, many of the books listed on page 162 contain useful design ideas.

If you don't have time to do more research into ways of planting, this book can be treated just like a cookery book, with each planting regarded as a single course. Your whole garden can be built up into a full-scale scheme by combining various plantings into an entire 'meal'. The notes to each photograph also suggest how the planting can be treated earlier, or later, in the season than at the time of the photograph. However, it is also possible to impose different plantings on top of each other, for good effects all season: for example, it would be an easy matter to put in the spring planting on page 30 along with the luscious colours of the summer planting on page 52.

This book concentrates mainly on plantings for early and high summer, the times when you will be most in the garden. Spring bedding, with its sheets of early colour (for example, the traditional mixture of tulips and wallflowers), looks better in parks than private gardens. The dazzling spring plantings so often photographed commonly have drifts of rare snowdrops, aconites, the delectable *Crocus tommassinianus*, or the inevitable daffodils, but they only work in big woodland gardens. In small gardens it is much simpler and less expensive to go for the charming look of spring plantings like the one on page 98.

Few of the gardens shown in this book make much use of rockeries, rose gardens, herb gardens, or even lawns. Obviously, you might want to have some or all of these, but many novice gardeners are often so eager to lay out their space that they do not think carefully enough about what they really want from it. They simply think of all the traditional garden 'elements' and look for somewhere to put them. And yet there is no point in having a rockery unless you care passionately about alpine plants (and many 'alpines' can be ravishingly pretty, though often tricky to grow), and even then it may be better to plant rock plants (or anything that needs sharp drainage) in a raised bed rather than in a traditional rockery. Likewise, the usual herb garden is a dull affair; most herbs run, sprawl, seed, or look dreadful planted between the spokes of a cartwheel. However, when herbs are mixed with vegetables or garden flowers (as on pages 141–154), lovely gardens can be created that will not only give you ample parsley, tarragon and sage for the kitchen, but will also be delightful places to sit. The same applies to rose gardens: almost every garden in the book has roses somewhere about it, but few of them have much that is modern, and almost none of them has a proper rose garden. Most have old or shrub roses integrated into the general planting, so that their owners do not have to look at bare ground dotted with the pruned and spiny shanks of modern bedding roses for much of the winter and early spring.

These missing garden elements apart, I hope that, from the plantings shown here and from some of the suggestions for putting them together and arranging the layout, you will be able to construct a garden to give you maximum delight in the shortest possible time.

How to use this book

Using the identification diagrams

The 'maps' identify the plants in the photograph. In some cases the planting is so simple that a map is unnecessary; in others the planting is so complex that some areas of the map cover a mix of plants listed. However, wherever possible, every plant that contributes to the feel of the planting is identified. Simply look for the relevant number on the photo-diagram, and that will give you the correct plant name that you will need when looking for the plant. The list on page 162 suggests books that give information about the conditions that the plant prefers, if any.

In a few cases, it has not been possible to identify the exact variety of a plant. Gardeners swap plants so much that names are often lost, and they also grow plants that, though they are in circulation between gardeners, have never been properly named, and are not available from nurseries. Where that has happened, I have suggested the most similar plant available. Sources for the plants in the photographs are given on page 155.

Using the ground plans

Many of the pictures also have a ground plan. In some cases these are based exactly on the photograph, suggest the number of plants needed for an initial planting (and to give a reasonably quick effect), and are intended for the smallest space that could be used to create the look of the planting. Some of the other planting plans are more loosely based on the pictures, largely where the plantings need to be modified for smaller gardens. These suggest alternative layouts, and sometimes additional plants (usually those from elsewhere in the same garden, so that the 'look' remains substantially similar).

If you want to use them, their scale is usually related to the area of garden photographed; mark out your ground as shown in the plan, and follow the indicated plant 'sites' for the number of plants you

need to grow or buy. Planting density is always a problem, as most new gardeners need quick effects and so plant too closely. Three to four plants are needed to achieve a clump comparable to that in the picture in two seasons or so.

The plans are only suggestions, and can easily be adapted to your own garden. It is important to try to keep the juxtapositions between plant types, though a good look at the photos will tell you if the plans are flexible. It should not be difficult to arrange it, and most of the plants will succeed in environments not identical to the ones pictured. If you want to transfer the plan exactly, make a copy of it and then draw over a grid of horizontal and vertical lines perhaps 2.5 cm (1 in) apart. In the garden, square the ground out with small sticks and plenty of thread or string to make a comparable grid. Then trace the design on to the soil with a trowel, and see how it looks. It is obviously much simpler if the grid in the garden is also square, although you could elongate the plan (rather than repeating the design as if it were wallpaper) by spacing the sticks out along one axis, as if you were stretching a rubber film. In some of the plans, the crosses indicate where plants should actually be planted if the clump needs several plants. If you stretch the plans, then you will need to add more.

In general, if the area to be filled is substantially larger than that covered by one of the plans, then it will look better if you put two or more plans together. For simplicity of effect (and usually greater elegance), use two identical plans, either side by side, or split one down the middle, and add halves to each end of the central plan area. Alternatively, mirror images of the layout added to either side of the plan will give you an attractive symmetrical planting (created on tracing paper, then transferred to the garden).

If you need to have plantings turning corners or bends, cut a diamond-shaped section out of the plan and paste that between sections of planting (alter the diamond's planting clumps to suit the space). As with more straightforward situations, complex ones can be squared out on the ground using pegs and builder's line. In general, though, this is unnecessary, and species-rich plantings like the ones on pages 37, 111 and 146 can be duplicated by any sensible mix of the plants they contain. They will often seed themselves around anyway, and equally prettily, in a season or two.

If you want to use two or more different plans in the same part of the garden, try to use those that harmonise and take into account the plants' requirements. Where possible, the text of each picture makes suggestions for linking it to other suites of plants. However, you do not have to be too precise about it: even major errors can look enchanting once planted.

Photographs and light

When choosing plantings from the photographs, it is worth bearing in mind that photography is pretty much a trick of the light. So if you see one of the gardens here (for the opening times of those that can be visited, see Appendix two), in another sort of light or at a different time of year, then it will not look exactly like the picture. It may be brighter or duller, or less or more lovely. You will, though, be able to see the whole thing, rather than merely the parts of the gardens photographed to represent my own preferences for certain sorts of garden (and not necessarily the parts that the owner likes best). The photographs also reflect my own preferences for certain groups of plants. So you won't see many dwarf conifers or ericas, whose lack of change through the season is, I think, the antithesis of gardening and its ephemeral beauties.

Planning your garden

Most of the photographs in this book are of herbaceous plants, and it is possible to have luxuriant plantings of these in the second or third season. The planting on page 82 is only a year old. However, a good part of the garden scene takes longer to achieve. The hedges and topiary in the garden on page 115, and the light woodland shown on pages 104 and 128, might take between seven and ten years to create, depending on the species

planted. To cover a wall with a planting like the one shown on page 136 might take five or six seasons, if you remember to feed the plants well; but you can still create luxuriant plantings like those on page 78 in only two summers.

It is important to be patient; there are plenty of things that grow much faster than the plants shown, and that would give you greenery in half the time, but you might regret it later, when you spend half your time in the garden rescuing other plants from the gloom they have created. This is particularly true of hedging. A good yew hedge might take three times as long to screen your garden, or part of it, from view, as the formidable Lawson's cypress, but it will look at least three times as good – and be a lot easier to maintain.

Light

People often worry about light levels and directions, and always ask us a lot of questions, giving precise details of wall heights, compass bearings and so on. Except for a few groups of plants (like camellias, whose flower buds are damaged by early morning sun after frost, and some early-flowering rhododendrons) aspect is not nearly as important as the total amount of light. Light levels vary with the season, and beds that look hopelessly shaded in winter can have surprising amounts of sun in summer when the sun is much higher in the sky. Plants are adaptable, and many of them can do well in what are apparently the 'wrong' conditions.

Light levels also depend on where you garden; erythroniums, that are supposed to like woodland shade and leafy soil, do wonderfully with us in Scotland in a hot dry angle of walls and in dreadful soil, but they might not do this in Sussex. In any case, shade is such a tremendous opportunity for planting lovely things – hostas, ferns, epimediums, heucheras, hellebores, tolmeias – that you should delight in it as much as in the sunniest corner of the garden. If you do not have any shade, try to create some – for your plants if not yourself. Shade also often implies privacy; European and North American urban gardens are often far more wooded than is common in Britain. A woodland garden (even with only three or four trees) can be marvellous on warm evenings, with a few candles. In some Scandinavian gardens, the only colour is provided by lushly planted tubs; the rest of the garden is paving beneath a canopy of foliage (giving a look rather like the charming garden on page 24).

Several of the gardens photographed here are quite heavily shaded. If you plant anything in the way of big shrubs or trees, you will find that shade increases quite fast, and that you might have to alter the garden flora to cope with this. If you decide to have a lawn, remember that most lawn seed contains grasses that like light. Though there are 'shade mixes' available, which can be successful, the grass is usually rather coarse. For a shaded small garden it might be better to pave as on page 24, or have paths through woodland vegetation as in the garden on page 98.

Soil

Many gardeners pay a great deal of attention to their soil, and there is a whole industry based on supplying kits for testing pH, fertility and so on. Few of the gardeners in these pages have paid much heed to these things since few of the plants they grow are fussy about the acidity or otherwise of the soil. Only if you want grand planting effects, especially if you want generous herbaceous borders like the ones on pages 75–93, or luxurious potagers like the one on page 146, will you need to learn about fertilisers and composts (see the bibliography on page 162), but gardens closer to the wild like those on pages 98–100 are virtually self-sustaining, and need very little attention. Techniques for soil preparation are given in the basic garden textbooks listed in the bibliography.

A few groups of plants do need special soil. Heathers, for example, hate chalky soil, while other plants hate acid soil. If you live on chalk downs in the South of England, or on a peaty hillside in Argyll, you might need specialised plantings not covered in this book. For less extreme conditions, say for gardens on London clay, sand, old field soil, and even sour town-garden soil, you will probably not need to do anything to the soil.

Digging is also often thought of as a bar to gardening by busy owners. Only the big herbaceous borders shown on pages 75–93 are dug over much – in their case every winter. None of the other plantings are treated like that, and many are too complicated to stick even a trowel in without damaging a bulb or interesting seedling. A number will need weeding, and a number will engender slugs and snails. These are not necessarily to be avoided, though hostas and delphiniums can be badly mutilated unless you have recourse to poisons. (See the section on wildlife on page 9.)

Layout and image

Because the photographs of the planting are showing gardens crammed to bursting point, they give little idea of how to organise or improve the spaces and vistas of your own garden. The layout design that will work best in your garden depends on a number of factors. You should consider not only the shape and size of your ground, but also how the garden is to be used. If you have children, consider how much space they need for playing, and what their requirements are for swings, sandpits, and the rest. How much space do you need for lounging around with a glass of wine on warm summer evenings? Do you adore lawnmowers so much that you must have plenty of lawn?

Once you have worked out the basic functions of your garden and the layout that they demand, a detailed plan can then be worked out, as well as the sort of 'look' that you want to create (whether you want an inner city courtyard, a country-cottage garden or a rival to Versailles). Work out what garden elements you have to have and want to have, not what you think you ought to have. As to layout detail, I personally like small intimate spaces in a garden, so would break anything large into smaller units (I hate mowing lawns). You, on the other hand, might prefer, or need, something more obviously spacious.

If you are dealing with a small garden, do not be trapped by the idea that small spaces need small plants – what they usually need is a few big ones. Overscaling always looks better than too much fuss. If, on the other hand, you could have vast lawns or open spaces, most of the plantings shown in this book will be lost if you string them out around the circumference. It is hard to concentrate on leaves and flowers if you are standing on the margin of three acres of grass, whereas it is not at all difficult if you are on a grass path only 3 m (10 ft) broad between borders. If you have the sort of house that needs to be set off by a sea of mown grass, give yourself a hedged flower garden against one side, or as near as you can without spoiling the view. Almost all the gardens shown in these pages are not especially large, but it is the density of their planting that gives most of them a feel of intimacy and great charm.

The gardens shown in this book vary considerably in their layouts. The one on page 104 has a series of narrow walks, formal and straight as well as woodland-like and winding, and both sorts of path traverse the entire space. There is a small lawn by the house, but it is not an important feature. On the other hand, in the garden on page 62 there is a biggish lawn, well away from the main plantings, and it is centred on a formal arrangement of sundial and roses. In almost none of the gardens shown, except the one on page 12, has the conventional scatter of island beds been dredged at random over a lawn, with wavy-edged borders surrounding it. Unless you have the skill of the owner of that garden (and even there, a slight feel of aimlessness applies to some parts of the design), the style is surprisingly difficult to make look effective. In a small space, with small beds, it can be particularly difficult.

The shape of the site is only really important in small gardens. If you have more space, you can easily create the shape of the garden within its boundaries. Whatever its size, bear in mind that you will be looking at it for most of the year from indoors. Most small gardens are rectangles, and their proportions must be considered, and the treatment of the boundaries particularly. Most gardeners think of dividing long narrow gardens into better shaped units; this can be very effective, but there are alternatives. For example, you could have a long herbaceous border or a woodland planting like the one on page 98, for the entire length of the garden, with no divisions, but with something nice to look at at the far end – a pretty greenhouse (a small conservatory with a brick back wall), or a nice seat or an arbour.

Slightly larger urban gardens can be more variable. 'L' shapes and triangles offer exciting possibilities for garden plans. Try to get a vista down the longest axis of the garden, even if this is not the one seen from the sitting-room windows: a long axis, with a seat or two, gives a sense of spaciousness. The much-vaunted concept of surprise can easily be met in ways other than having curving paths that lead nowhere and all the usual tricks. In any case, it will soon surprise only visitors, whereas good planting will give you, the owner, pleasure all the time.

In small rectangular spaces, clothe the walls or fences as in the photograph on page 124, and choose the ground planting to suit the light levels and your needs (herbs for the kitchen, or a few vegetables, or flowers for the house, or whether you use the garden only in the evenings, or alone, or with friends and family).

In towns, many front gardens are just paving, railings, and perhaps a small pot with a sad geranium in it, but they could be much more interesting. Even in modern housing estates where there are restrictions on plant heights, it is easy to do something fun and pretty. In general, as front gardens are not very private, and so working in them is less pleasant, keep to low-maintenance plantings. If you have a basement with an 'area', use sections of shade plantings in big pots or, if there is some sun, use some of the potfuls shown on pages 66–72.

The back garden is the place for enjoyment, whether it is devoted to vegetables and grass, to a sophisticated orchard, to elegant arrangements of herbaceous flowers or to a patio – which does not have to be the standard concoction of concrete slabs, white plastic planters, and colourful hanging baskets (see pages 24–42).

New gardeners often worry about whether to have a formal or an informal garden. Most of the gardens shown in this book make use of straight lines and the formal vistas that they allow. This is partly also my own preference, gardening as we do in a series of rectangular walled enclosures. However, it is also the preference of many good planters, who find the formal framework makes a better foil to their plants than island beds. Most of the informal gardens in this book are those where the terrain itself is unsuited to formal layouts without great expense. Most small modern gardens are rectangular, so the formal framework is already set up and can easily be exploited.

I have tried to keep the plantings shown in this book fairly democratic. Perfect planting is perfect planting, wherever it can be found, and the plantings in this book, while they may be in the gardens of grand houses, will look just as pretty in inner-city gardens. For example, the enticing tangle of roses and alliums at Balbithan House (page 128), or even Broughton Castle (page 57), would look every bit as lovely in front of a modern house. The country garden on page 100, wild and wooded, is duplicated by the owner in his other tiny garden in the middle of London. The garden shown in the photograph on page 52 is apparently urban in its sophistication, but is actually to be found in a rural part of Dorset. So, do as you please: all you have to do is have fun imagining (or image making) the garden. Most of the gardeners in this book have had fun outwitting the conventions. Above all, try not to cram too many garden features into a small space, but do a few things well. If you want a pool, but have a tiny garden, you could fill the whole plot with water and plant it like the one on page 35; you could have it like the delightful wild orchard on page 98; or pave the centre and plant the margins, like the garden on page 50.

Cost

Cost can also limit what you do. Few of the plants found in these pages cost very much: many are cheaply bought from garden centres or nurseries; a good number can be grown even more cheaply from seed. Even if you can only afford one *Hosta tokudama* 'Aureo-nebulosa', or *Ligularia przewalskii*, it will eventually grow into a clump that can be divided and replanted to look even more grand. However, this will take longer than spending more money and buying things in threes, sixes, or dozens. It is always better not to skimp, so if you have a limited budget for the garden, it is usually a

wise idea to work on a small piece at a time and make it look good, while keeping the rest under grass, or at least free of weeds. After many years of trying, we still have plenty of space in our garden that is not yet properly planted.

However cheap plant luxury might be if you can put the time into it all, it is the paths and other hard surfaces, garden 'props' and so on, that cost, on the whole, a lot more. Some of these are essential to the enjoyment and style of your garden. In general, you get what you pay for, but you can still enjoy your garden with a seat made from two bits of tree stump and a plank (which would actually suit many of the gardens in these pages perfectly) rather than something antique, Italian and solid marble.

Seating is the most basic of the garden props, and although a seat is always an attractive way to give point to a vista, the view from the seat itself may not be so good. As well as 'design' seating, ensure that there are lesser seats where the view is good, or where the sun falls at breakfast, or finishes up on a summer evening. Even in a cool climate, sitting outdoors is one of the great pleasures of having a garden. Permanent seating is best; having to fish something musty out of the garage to sit on is one of the most inhibiting things about gardening. If necessary, design the planting about each seat to suit the time of day: for example, night-scented stocks and *Mirabilis jalapa* for seating areas used after 4 o'clock in the afternoon.

A list of suppliers of interesting garden props can be found in the *Guide to the Specialist Nurseries and Garden Suppliers of Britain and Ireland*, edited by Sarah Cotton (see bibliography). Other good sources can be local junk or antique sales, though garden props now often fetch high prices, or try local craftsmen. Even so, plants can look fine in old tin cans.

Because this book is focused as strongly as possible on the plants themselves, there are few illustrations of some of the nicest garden props of all: loggias, summerhouses and greenhouses. Quite a few of the gardens here do have them, whether they are made from timber yard waste and a few poles (making a lovely place to sit and chat after dusk) as in the garden on page 153, or grand eighteenth-century mini-temples. They all give such pleasure that even the tiniest garden should have some sort of shelter in it, even if it is only a shed with an extended roof. In the north, it could even be enclosed with glazed doors and have some form of heating – which would make it a marvellous place to sit even in winter.

Planting and maintenance

Buying plants, or a packet of seed, is easy, and getting the plants or seedlings into the ground is not much harder. However, plants and plantings do have certain requirements before they will give you as much pleasure as they can.

Many of these lovely plantings are composed of a mix of trees, shrubs, and herbaceous plants. It is tempting to plant everything at once, and hope that the photographs come alive quickly and easily. Alas, it does not work like that (we've tried). If you possibly can, plant the trees and shrubs first, leave for a season or two, then put in the herbaceous plants. If you don't manage to do this, make sure that the slower-growing things, especially young shrubs, are not swamped by the lush growth of the more opportunistic annuals and perennials. Otherwise, they won't thrive as they should, and the effect you want will be much delayed.

If you have bought plants growing in containers, you won't need to get them into the ground immediately. In any case, it is sometimes worth keeping them in pots for a bit, so that you can set them out on the ground you want to plant. That way, you'll soon have a rough idea of how they should be spaced, and how they will look once grown. Minor adjustments are easily made. They will, though, need watering assiduously. If you're unsure about how to plant them, have a look at some of the books suggested in the bibliography. Plant as well as you have time for; early work means early luxury.

Only fifty per cent or so of the plants shown in these pages will be available from your local garden centre. You will have either to visit nurseries, or buy by mail order. Page 155 contains lists of plant suppliers, but these are far from exhaustive; many other nurseries will stock most of the plants included in this book. If you want a wider range, refer to a book called *The Plant Finder* (see bibliography). Nurseries change their stock fairly frequently, both to keep their public interested and as their waves of propagation fail or succeed. Always ask for a current catalogue before sending off an order, so that you can check on a plant's availability. You will also find differences in price. Don't necessarily buy the cheapest. When sending for catalogues, it will help the nursery stay in business if you enclose a few stamps and a large envelope; write your name and address clearly. (You can always phone, though most nurserymen are too busy to chat to you about your garden, and will almost always lose the piece of paper on which they scribbled your address.) Though a few gardeners may be disappointed with plants bought by post, most nurserymen will be keen to keep your business, and will send plants as large and healthy as possible for the price.

It is also worth looking through seed lists, but quite a few plant varieties with special names will not come 'true' from seed, and so the final effect may not look the same. Do not select rarer variants of any of the species described unless you know what you are doing. I visited a number of gardens, new ones especially, where rarity had been more than a little confused with beauty. The wonderful herbaceous borders on page 78 are made with the simplest of flowers.

Aftercare is also essential. Newly planted herbaceous species take a month or more to become properly established, and will need a check kept on their well-being for at least that long, especially during dry weather. Any sign of flagging leaves needs instant work with the watering can or the hose. New shrubs and trees will need cosseting for the whole of their first year with you.

Beginner gardeners worry a great deal about pruning and thinning. Only a few of the gardens here need much skill at these, though you will need to learn about fruit pruning if you want to have a potager – though it isn't in the least difficult. We never prune (or spray) the fruit trees in our garden, but we still have more fruit than we can eat. Most of the pruning done in the gardens shown in these pages is merely keeping the paths clear in a reasonably elegant way. This usually involves thinning plants of branches or stems, rather than clipping them like a hedge. Anything that needs special treatment is noted in the text; everything else is perfectly easy.

Another aspect of garden maintenance is weeding. The density of most of the plantings here is too high to allow the use of a hoe or weedkiller; you will have to hand weed during the early growth of the planting. However, once the decorative plants are fully grown, weeds will not become established easily: the garden plants offer so much competition that any weeds that do germinate will have a struggle to survive. Some weeding will always be necessary, however, but many gardeners find weeding relaxing and therapeutic.

A great deal of experience and effort has gone into almost all the gardens shown here, and the owners often work hard at keeping the plantings in the sort of shape they like (and that means, except in the wildest gardens, free of weeds). The only work that this book tries to save you is the part concerned with learning what plants look nice with what. If you find yourself seduced by some of the more lavish plantings shown here (and I hope you will), particularly some of the herbaceous borders, then you will be committed to some really hard work. However, the end result can be thrilling, and easily repay the effort that goes into them a hundredfold.

Perfect plantings and wildlife

Ecological gardens in these pages include any of the semi-wild ones, and apparently low-maintenance ones. Ecology, of course, can be annoying too. The owner of the one on page 30 complains that badgers eat his tulip bulbs, though he prefers to let the badgers do just that. The roses in a number of gardens shown are regularly cropped by deer. However, in almost all of them, the drone of bees, the rattle of dragonflies and the softer flutter of moths and butterflies is common. Erica beds, beds of modern roses, and dwarf conifers will give you nothing at all.

However, 'ecology' will also include snails, slugs, aphids and fungi. In general, though you may lose some rose buds to mildew, greenfly and sawflies, and holes will appear in almost everything else, not too much is needed to keep things in order. If you want standard gooseberry bushes in your parterre or potager, you will have to spray, or every leaf will vanish. If you plant sheets of roses, keep an eye out for chafers and caterpillars; every bud can be destroyed. Rabbits really do need to be fenced out properly, or shot (there is a rabbit-proof flora, which is interesting, but I didn't find any good schemes made from it – though that would be possible) and deer can also be a great nuisance in the country. The owner of the garden on page 24 said that he wasn't bothered by snails; the peacocks ate them. If you don't have peacocks, and you like box hedges, you will need anti-snail chemicals. We once collected two stone of snails in a single evening from 50 yards of hedging. You will have to spray violas and violets against greenfly or you will lose your plants. Do remember that the larvae of all the showier insects you want to attract usually eat something nice in the garden; so having wildlife will often also mean lots of holes in your leaves. And if you're determined to have a potager, keep a look out for all the major vegetable pests.

'Companion plantings' (where certain flowers and herbs are planted between rows of vegetables to deter pests) in potagers can often look pretty, but even to an unbiased friend, whose delightfully rustic potager is on page 141, they seem to have only marginal effects. However, keep trying and see what works. Potagers are inimical to wildlife. Almost every bird on the wing and every rodent in the hedgerow will be eyeing it greedily. And, come late summer, every small boy in the neighbourhood will be after even the sourest of apples.

However even the tiniest space is packed with potential. A tiny formal garden, planted with lavenders, hyssops, stocks and wallflowers, will attract every bee and butterfly for miles. In a garden with herbs, almost all the herbs are good for this too, though beware of thyme carpets on turf seats or on patios: they become carpets of bees.

A note on the pictures

Not all the gardens shown can be visited (for the opening times of those that are, see Appendix two). One or two of them are not identified at the owner's request.

A note on the plant names

In the plant lists the Latin names have been given in most cases, followed by the cultivar name, and the common name in brackets, to help with identification and purchase.

The Front Garden

The traditional idea developed in the 1850s of front gardens as tiny pieces of lawn, surrounded by flower beds and a few shrubs, isn't necessarily the most exciting one. A dense planting, perhaps with smallish trees right by the house, can give a much more exciting and romantic approach as well as screening the house from neighbours, passers-by and the street. Dense planting can also reduce the effect of street noise, though it will mean a slight loss of light from front ground-floor rooms (although deciduous trees will allow plenty of winter light, if you can cope with fallen leaves).

North American and continental European suburbs are always much more leafy than British ones, and even in deep shade lovely plantings are possible. Many old town gardens have high stone or brick walls which are perfect for mixes of climbers. In modern housing developments, divisions between gardens are more likely to be low timber fences or wires tautened between posts, which also offer good planting opportunities. Before you rush out to buy a hundred 'Leylandii' conifers, consider using a stout trellis to support climbers. Use treated laths measuring at least 2.5 x 20 cm (1 x 8 in), spaced at 30 cm (12 in) intervals – nailed vertically and horizontally – and well supported on 10 x 10 cm (4 x 4 in) posts. Metal post-holders are simpler to use than concrete for securing the posts, and easier to replace if needed. In small spaces, a planted trellis will take up much less room than a hedge (especially of conifers), take less out of the ground, and give you a great deal more pleasure. It will give you privacy just as quickly. It is possible to buy trellis panels in fancy architectural designs, often painted dazzling white or bright green. Lovely in shop window displays or as a restaurant fitting, they can, however, be rather dominating in a garden.

Planting 1 Lighting up a shaded garden

Even a restricted range of plants, in clever hands, can create rich and subtle effects. Here, using only three genera, Beth Chatto has made a luxuriant tapestry of golden foliage, and one which gives pleasure from early spring to the first hard frosts. The golden-leaved raspberry is a perfect foil for three kinds of hosta, and the essentially golden effect is counterpointed by a scattering of bluebells.

Developments and the seasons In a small garden, you might need to have some other spring flowers besides bluebells: for early in the season, it would be tempting to have white daffodils such as 'Thalia' or 'Mount Hood'. For late summer when the hostas are in flower, you could add some white or soft purplish pink astilbes, and a couple of tufts of a good hardy fern like *Matteuccia struthiopteris* or *Dryopteris filix-mas*. A wall behind could be draped with white roses, or the mauvish rose 'Veilchenblau'. Clumps of September-flowering *Aster macrophylla*, with its spiky amethyst blooms and handsome heart-shaped leaves, could be added at each side of the planting.

Site This would make an excellent scheme for a small and shady front garden with gravel or flagstone paths. It could tolerate a few hours' sun a day, but needs some shade from an overhead tree, such as a native birch, or a green-leaved, white-flowered prunus. Do not plant the yellow *Robinia pseudo-acacia* 'Frisia' here, or you might find the golden effect overdone.

Maintenance and costs Once established, these ground-cover plants keep maintenance to a minimum.

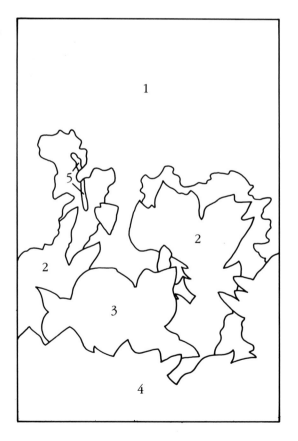

1 *Rubus idaeus* 'Aurea' (golden-leaved raspberry)
2 *Hosta fortunei* 'Aurea'
3 *Hosta fortunei* 'Albo Picta'
4 *Hosta fortunei* 'Marginato Alba'
5 *Hyacinthoides non-scripta* (bluebell)

Props and additions Some big pots containing soft grey-blue *Nierembergia frutescens*, or the marvellous pinkish tan flowers and sticky green leaves of *Mimulus cupreus*, could be placed nearby. In denser shade, use a plant with good leaves instead, mixing, for example, a red-speckled mimulus with the wonderful *Hosta sieboldiana*.

Substitutions The rubus is lovely, but may be difficult to find. A similar effect could be achieved using either the golden-leaved form of philadelphus (*P. coronarius* 'Aurea') or golden weigela. The hostas are harder to substitute: try the easy 'Golden Flash' and 'Flamboyance' for the yellows, or look for the marvellous 'Frances Williams' for the green

variegated one. Instead of the little touches of purplish blue of the bluebells, you could plant a scattering of the green-leaved blue-flowered form of the low-growing *Ajuga reptans* (bugle), or, if you want to stick to bulbs, put in a dozen or so *Camassia leichtlinii* (quamash) which has tall rockets of soft blue stars. For late summer, you could add contrast with a few plants of the shrieking strawberry pink of *Potentilla nepalensis* 'Miss Willmott'.

Ideas for its use This planting would also suit a tiny courtyard, but using a philadelphus rather than the raspberry. You could either plant right up to the paving, or add a border of an ivy like 'Green Ripple', with dark green leaves and waved edges.

Planting 2 Cottage abundance for a shady bed

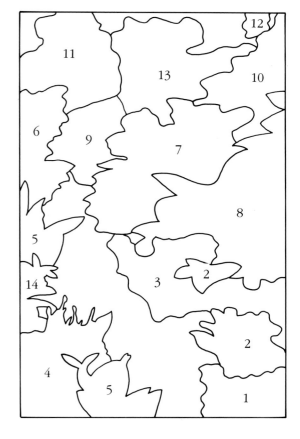

1 *Bellis* 'Dresden China' (double daisy)
2 *Myosotis* seedlings (forget-me-not)
3 *Brunnera macrophylla* 'Variegata'
4 *Ranunculus ficaria* 'Anemone flowered'
5 *Rumex sanguineus* 'Sanguineus' (bloody dock)
6 *Dicentra formosa* 'Alba' (Dutchman's breeches)
7 *Meconopsis cambrica* orange form (Welsh poppy)
8 *Mandragora officinalis* (mandrake)
9 *Tiarella grandiflora*
10 *Lunaria annua* (honesty)
11 *Corydalis lutea*
12 *Euphorbia characias*
13 *Galeobdolon argentatum*
14 *Crocus* 'Snow Bunting'

David Bromley, an obsessive gardener and plants-man, still has room in his ravishing Shropshire garden for the weedy and the self-sown. This early summer mixture of honesty, forget-me-nots, and Welsh poppies is combined with some grander plants – mandrake, brunnera, and white Dutch-man's breeches – to make a delightful, sophisti-cated and long-lasting planting. If the plants of the bloody dock are well fed, they produce some splendid foliage for cutting.

Developments and the seasons   Everything here flowers fairly early in the season, but for an even earlier start you could add some double snowdrops, even rare ones like the double yellow-ish 'Lady Elphinstone'. Later on in summer, the daisy will still be flowering, and you'll have lovely seed pods from the honesty. The flowers of the mandrake are sinister; the seed pods grand.

Site   This planting requires dampish shade, with only a little direct sunlight.

Maintenance and cost   Only the brunnera will cost much; the rest, bar the daisy and the dicentra, will do as seed, and will seed themselves around prettily thereafter. The daisy needs an occasional spray against greenfly.

Props and additions   Though some of the plants are grand, the general effect of the planting is of cottage abundance. Any additions could usefully augment the same idea, for example an old earthenware pot could be filled with a striking fern like *Dryopteris cristata* or with variegated ginger mint.

Substitutions   The sharp pink of the daisy is important; the only other daisy of similar shape is 'Alice', though packet seedlings might produce something suitable. The variegation of the brunnera gives another good colour accent, as well as nice early blue flowers. The creamy white dicentra could be substituted by rarities like the lovely yellow *Corydalis cheilanthifolia*, with its wonder-fully cut foliage (it runs less badly, flowers most of the summer and it seeds itself well in locations like this), or perhaps a white *Dicentra spectabilis* (bleeding heart).

Ideas for its use   This planting is much deeper than the photograph suggests, and would make a charming bed on either side of a slightly wider brick path to a suitably cottage-like house. It would also make a charming underplanting beneath gnarled rose bushes or lightly shading, deep-rooted trees.

Planting 3 Warm colours for a warm corner

Two seasons before this photograph was taken, in June, this tiny, sunny front garden was baldly flagged with stone. The flags were needed somewhere else, so the newly cleared ground was filled with plants chosen for a quick effect, as we didn't have time to do much else to it. The earth has now disappeared beneath the plants shown here, as well as euphorbia, eglantine, and double Scots rose.

Developments and the seasons In early spring, aconites and pale yellow crocuses (such as the dwarf species *Crocus susianus* or cloth-of-gold crocus, which is heavily honey-scented) are in flower in this bed, and in late summer there are various late-flowering yellow day lilies, and tiger lilies. For September, you could add *Anthemis tinctoria* varieties along with *Inula hookeri* and a scattering of white *Anemone hupehensis*.

Site This planting succeeds on poor soil and in the partial shade of stone walls. It is a windy site: the yellow iris is occasionally blown over. It could be reproduced in any not too shady, not too damp, area.

Maintenance and cost Almost everything here is cheap, even free, if you have friends with seed. The only rare thing is the chelidonium, although even that is becoming easier to find. In the shadow is a yellow Scots rose (*Rosa spinosissima*) and the delectable 'Bowles Golden' grass (a variety of *Milium effusum*) – both of which could be omitted.

Substitutions Everything here is easy to get hold of, except perhaps the bearded iris 'Scintilla', but a good substitute would be 'Blue Denim' (altering the colour balance a little), or 'Green Spot'. The artemisia could be replaced by another variety such as 'Valerie Finnis', or even the herbaceous *Artemisia ludoviciana* – but the shrubby species are just as easy to maintain. The ivy 'Goldheart' would do instead of the 'Aurea Angulata', but is less subtly colourful. The oak-leaved variant of the chelidonium, though less good than this one, is pretty too, with larger, simpler flowers.

Props and additions Out of the picture are more yellow roses: the marvellous shrub rose 'Cantabrigensis', adrift with soft yellow flowers in early July, and with red lacquer hips in September. More easily available yellow roses which could be used are 'Mermaid' or 'Golden Showers', both climbers. Tubs and pots of *Lilium longiflorum*, the Easter lily (easily grown from seed), or a mixture of *Bidens ferulaefolius* and *Helichrysum petiolatum* would also work well. The *Argyranthemum frutescens*, or Paris daisy, called 'Jamaica Primrose' would be good, though the closely related *A. arguta*, with its blue-green leaves, would be better still.

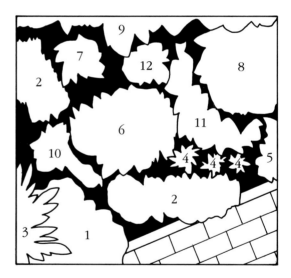

1 *Melissa officinalis* 'Aurea' (golden balm)
2 *Chelidonium maius* 'Laciniata'
3 *Hemerocallis lilio-asphodelus* (day lily)
4 *Lilium tigrinum* (tiger lily)
5 *Iris* 'Scintilla'
6 *Artemisia* 'Powys Castle'
7 *Meconopsis cambrica* (Welsh poppy)
8 *Rosa eglanteria* (eglantine)
9 *Hedera helix* 'Aurea Angulata' (common ivy)
10 *Potentilla argyrophylla* 'Atrosanguinea'
11 *Iris* pale cream form
12 *Aquilegia* 'Nora Barlow'

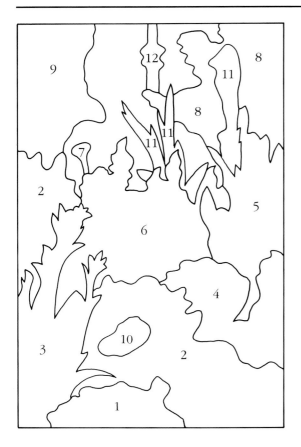

1 *Melissa officinalis* 'Aurea' (golden balm)
2 *Chelidonium maius* 'Laciniata'
3 *Hemerocallis lilio-asphodelus* (day lily)
4 *Lilium tigrinum* (tiger lily)
5 *Iris* 'Scintilla'
6 *Artemisia* 'Powys Castle'
7 *Meconopsis cambrica* (Welsh poppy)
8 *Rosa eglanteria* (eglantine)
9 *Hedera helix* 'Aurea Angulata' (common ivy)
10 *Potentilla argyrophylla* 'Atrosanguinea'
11 *Iris* pale cream form
12 *Aquilegia* 'Nora Barlow'

Ideas for its use   All these plants do well on poor soil, and so the planting would be suitable for the base of a fairly hot and sunny wall. The golden balm and the eglantine have splendidly perfumed leaves, and the day lilies smell good too. Try it on the sunny side of a patio, especially if it is of flagstones or good reddish bricks.

Planting 4 Cool harmonies in white and pink

On a wet silvery-grey late summer afternoon the gardens at Vann, partly created by Gertrude Jekyll, are very romantic. The planting shown here was done by the house's owners – and how much more enjoyable it is than the average front garden. None of the plants is itself grand, and a number are self-sown, but they are put together in a satisfying way that gives pleasure all season, and makes the front garden a delightful place in which to linger.

Developments and the seasons   To give colour in spring and early summer, add tulips in purplish pinks, white, and yellow (for example, the yellow lily-flowered ones on page 30), mixed with a few honesty plants (*Lunaria annua*). The planting on page 24 might suggest other possible additions; and *Hesperis matronalis*, the sweet rocket, with white or pale purple flowers, could also be added to perfume the garden in early summer.

Site   Shelter from strong winds, partial shade and a loamy, moisture-retentive soil would be the optimum conditions for most of these plants, but they will succeed in a wide variety of situations. A peaty soil would be helpful, but is not essential.

Maintenance and cost   Maintenance involves making sure that the creeper doesn't swamp the gutters and windows, and that the jasmines are not too shaded in order that they flower well. To keep the path clear, the hydrangeas, in particular, will need regular thinning. You could alter the colours of the hydrangeas by using aluminium sulphate (or

1 *Anemone hupehensis* (Japanese anemone)
2 *Hedera helix* 'Silver Queen' (common ivy)
3 *Hypericum androsaemum* (St John's wort)
4 *Jasminum nudiflorum* (winter-flowering jasmine)
5 *Oenothera biennis* (evening primrose)
6 *Hydrangea* 'Bouquet Rose'
7 *Hydrangea* 'Lanarth White'
8 *Jasminum stephanense* (pink jasmine)
9 *Dryopteris filix-mas* (male fern)
10 *Parthenocissus quinquefolia* (Virginia creeper)
11 *Buxus sempervirens* (common box)
12 Dock
    A scattering of the wild *Myosotis arvensis*
    (forget-me-not)

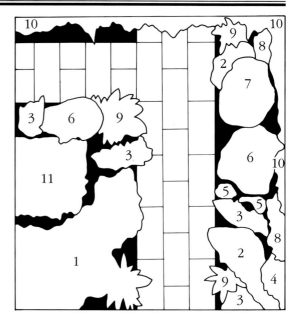

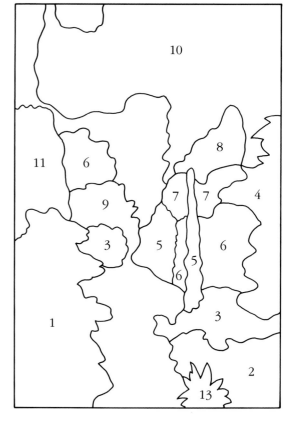

commercial 'blueing agent', the same, but more expensive). Blue hydrangeas would perhaps go better with the yellow flowers, and would, once the colour softens at the end of the season, look marvellous in front of the creeper. The creeper is self-clinging and the pink jasmine will twine through it, but the winter-flowering jasmine needs to be tied into its support.

Props and additions   This rather wild and very pretty garden would be more highly scented with the addition of a few pots of lilies by the doorway (the ordinary *Lilium regale* would be perfectly good), and a big tubful of night-scented stock, whose dull lilac flowers would be just the right colour (but as the flowers are closed during the day combine it with a verbena such as 'Silver Anne').

Substitutions   If you want something a little less subdued in colour, you could change the anemones for *Anemone hupehensis* 'Lady Gilmour', which is a rich rosy purple with shaggy petals. You could also use other, more brightly coloured hydrangeas. Later in the season everything here will be dominated by the lacquered scarlet leaves of the Virginia creeper, and so you might prefer the white- and pink-variegated leaves of *Parthenocissus henryana* (Chinese Virginia creeper), which drapes itself elegantly and hugs the house with less determination. For more colour below, you might add some dusky mauve *Verbascum phoeniceum*, which would also self-sow. If you have enough sun, the sword-shaped leaves of irises would add an architectural element; the beardless *Iris unguicularis* would also give late winter flowers in shades of blue, while *I. lazica*, with similar flowers, would be a good choice if the border is especially narrow.

Ideas for its use   This planting could easily be adapted to provide a border at the end of a garden, under overgrown trees. The creepers could also be grown up a trellis or wire-netting fences, although they need plenty of height to look good.

Patios and Courtyards

In small urban gardens, it is usually a waste of time to have a tiny lawn to match – it never looks right, and is often worn and scrawny. You also need somewhere to store a lawn mower, and something to do with the clippings. It is better by far to have paving, and turn your garden into a courtyard. It is important to choose the paving material carefully: many kinds of artificial slab are unattractive, particularly those made of coloured concrete. It is possible to find good colours of concrete paviour, and some of the ones that imitate riven stone can look reasonably good. Best of all (though very expensive) are second-hand paving stones, or even the sorts of Caithness flags once used for paving kitchens and halls. (Sandstone flags, being more porous, can become very slippery if you let algae grow.)

Cobbles or engineering brick are cheaper than paving, and can be just as attractive. Antique paviours from old stables and cattle courts can also look excellent if relaid with care. Great fun can be had with the design of the paving pattern, and the patterns almost always work well with an abundance of plants.

Gravel is a cheaper alternative to paving, but needs more maintenance. 'River washed' gravel in the smallest size available makes the most sympathetic surface. Crushed stone gravel can grate when walked on, and some of the colours, from dead grey to sinister reds, look unattractive in the garden, but if you can find no alternative, use the smallest grade you can. The best way of making quick and effective gravel paths and seating areas is to put down a special woven nylon sheeting called 'Lobrene' (big garden centres or builders' merchants sell various grades), cover it with 2–3 cm (1 in) or so of coarse builders' sand, and then a 2–3 cm (1 in) layer of gravel. Using a thicker layer of gravel gives paths that are far too much like shingle beaches, and just as hard to walk upon.

The basic plants round a courtyard should be structural. Do not be wary of plants that give shade; some dappled shade from high-pruned trees can be just as much of a delight as strong sunshine, especially in spring and autumn. It is also pleasant, in high summer, to sit out in the evening beneath, and among, plenty of foliage. Enclosure can be exciting. In winter, good plant architecture, interesting tree trunks especially, or good evergreen leaves, are essential. Look also at maples and birches for smallish trees, and don't necessarily buy everything with the varietal name 'Contorta' that you see (almost all are horrible). There are some good evergreen plantings in the photographs in this section. It is worth having good architectural foliage lower down too; all the hellebores, for instance, and especially *Helleborus corsicus*, are excellent in this respect, and genera like acanthus, some of the bergenias, and the evergreen sorts of pulmonaria, are also good. There is no reason why winter should be dull.

Keep the planting dense. In a tiny paved space, rather than try for colour in the ground – bedding, or shrubs – stick to good greenery, like that on page 24, and add colour in tubs, pots, troughs and other containers. In large urban gardens it is also possible to wrap herbaceous borders like those on page 75 around the paving, and really live among the flowers.

Planting 5 Green serenity in a walled garden

Alan and Neil Roger's walled garden in Wester Ross in Scotland has so much of interest that it was difficult to choose the best parts. It is divided into a series of often quite small garden rooms, all handsomely planted and populated by tribes of peacocks (which keep down the slugs and snails). In one of the smaller gardens I found this simple foliage planting which, because much of it is evergreen, would look as serene in December as in June.

Developments and the seasons   If your garden is so small that this can be your only planting, the seasons are best marked by a good selection of pink and white flowers in pots or tubs, for example fragrant white hyacinths for spring (get doubles if you can), and for summer, standard fuchsias (the long narrow-flowered sorts like 'Thalia' or *Fuchsia fulgens*), acid-pink geraniums (like the stunning netted-leaved 'White Mesh'), heavily fed pots of hostas and *Francoa ramosa*. If a corner of the garden has enough sun, lilies (pink *L. speciosus* would be good), the annual *Mirabilis jalapa* ('Marvel of Peru') and maroon nicotianas, or the stately white *Nicotiona sylvestris*, could be grown.

Site   These plants will all thrive in shade, and so you could plant them beneath biggish trees, mature lilacs or some of the grandly scaled buddleias such as *Buddleia colvillei*, if your garden is in a mild district, or *B. globosa* (both grown elsewhere in this garden) if it is not. This view would be endlessly satisfying seen through French windows or patio doors. Even in winter the skimmias would look good, and the props give colour. Cobbles, bricks or flags might look rather better than these slabs.

Maintenance and cost   This planting would not cost much, and maintenance consists mainly of keeping the skimmias from enclosing you too tightly. The fern leaves will go brown in autumn, but do not need to be cut down until the spring. The bonsai maple will need careful watering.

Props and additions   The simple benches and tables are of concrete, but stools or chairs of almost any sort would do. Ceramic garden seats, which are now widely imported, would look good, especially in 'famille rose' colours. For a quick bonsai effect, buy young Japanese maples and put them in oriental-looking pots. The hard surfaces could be margined with scillas, or even the common bluebell.

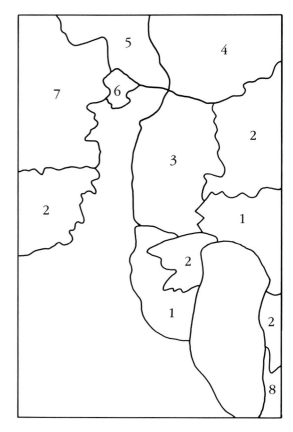

1 *Hedera colchica* 'Variegata'
2 *Dryopteris filix-mas*
3 *Skimmia japonica* 'Rubella'
4 *Salix* species
5 *Pyrus salicifolia* 'Alba'
6 *Chamaecyparis obtusa* 'Aurea' (bonsai)
7 *Choisya japonica*
8 *Allium* species

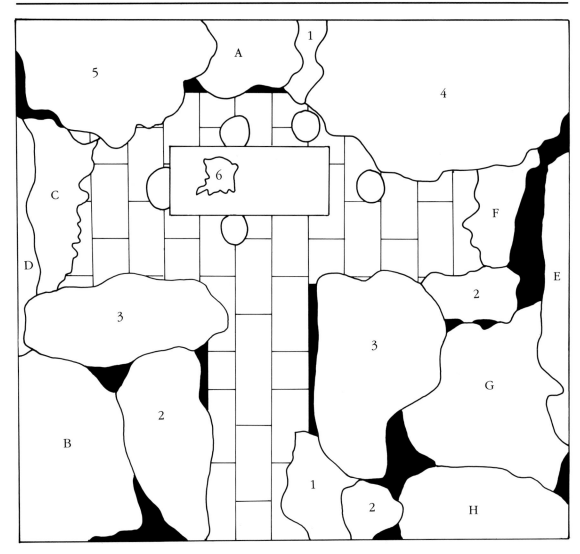

1 *Hedera colchica* 'Variegata'
2 *Dryopteris filix-mas*
3 *Skimmia japonica* 'Rubella'
4 *Salix* species
5 *Pyrus salicifolia* 'Alba'
6 *Chamaecyparis obtusa* 'Aurea' (bonsai)
7 *Choisya japonica*
8 *Allium* species

ON PLAN ONLY
A *Daphne mezereum* with *Aster macrophylla*
B A white lilac underplanted with *Aruncus sylvester*
C *Hosta* 'Frances Williams'
D *Hedera helix* 'Parsley Crested'
E *Hydrangea petiolaris*
F *Hemerocallis lilio-asphodelus*
G *Philadelphus* 'Belle Etoile'
H *Buddleia fallowiana*

Substitutions   Nothing here is hard to find except for the bonsai maple, but you could 'make' your own (see page 24). Only the props provide colour, though they do not necessarily have to be grand and oriental as they are here. Seats and tables painted blue and glazed pots for bonsai trees or other plants will give the same general effect.

Ideas for its use   The serene sense of enclosure suggests a lovely peaceful courtyard – somewhere for quiet musing, and candlelight at night.

Planting 6 Leafy elegance for damp shade

1 *Hosta* 'Thomas Hogg'
2 *Ligularia przewalskii*
3 *Tovara* 'Painter's Palette'
4 *Bergenia* 'Ballawley' hybrid
5 *Iris foetidissima* 'Variegata' (stinking iris)

6 *Alchemilla mollis* (lady's mantle)
7 *Rodgersia aesculifolia*
8 *Camassia leichtlinii* 'Atropurpurea'
9 *Wisteria japonica* white form
10 *Mentha rotundifolia* 'Variegata'

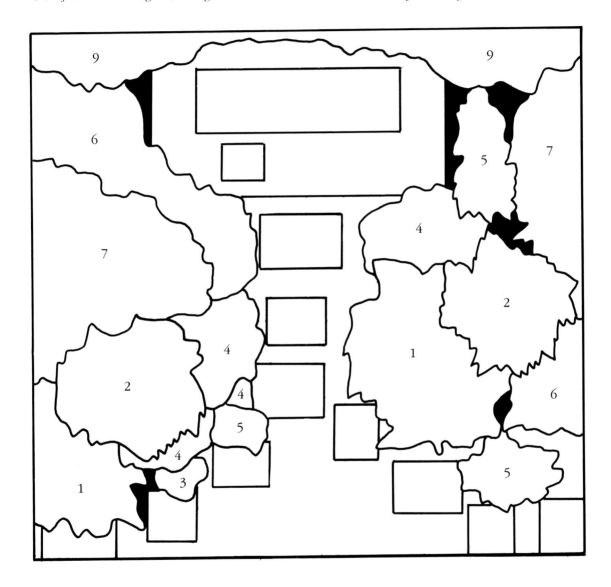

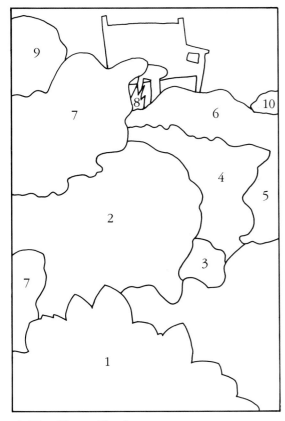

1 *Hosta* 'Thomas Hogg'
2 *Ligularia przewalskii*
3 *Tovara* 'Painter's Palette'
4 *Bergenia* 'Ballawley' hybrid
5 *Iris foetidissima* 'Variegata' (stinking iris)
6 *Alchemilla mollis* (lady's mantle)
7 *Rodgersia aesculifolia*
8 *Camassia leichtlinii* 'Atropurpurea'
9 *Wisteria japonica* white form
10 *Mentha rotundifolia* 'Variegata'

This marvellous assemblage of strong foliage, photographed in July, shows how good planting can transform a small, damp shaded space and turn what is so often a gardener's forgotten zone into somewhere that gives pleasure all season. It is as if the flower arranger's art has been applied to this fine planting, and the key element is the juxtaposition of the marvellous ligularia with other, simpler foliage. The planting is actually beside a shaded mill pond, and the bold variegation of the hosta works marvellously in the watery light.

Developments and the seasons Here, snowdrops start the season, though white or pale blue sweet violets could be added to set off the bergenia flowers. The addition of *Camassia leichtlinii*, with its spiky blue flowers, would give colour later in the season. Since everything here gives good autumn foliage, flowers are not needed then.

Site The base of a north-facing wall, if you can ensure sufficient moisture, would be suitable. It would also be perfect beside a small formal pool, perhaps under a winter-flowering cherry, *Prunus subhirtella* 'Autumnalis'.

Maintenance and cost The alchemilla will seed itself exuberantly, and needs careful thinning. The lovely iris grows slowly and needs protecting from the rampant bergenia. None of the plants is expensive.

Props and additions For some added transient colour, you could keep it subtle with big pots of the ornamental ginger mint or a large pale mimulus like 'San Francisco', or add brightness with the narrow coral-red flowers of *Mimulus cardinalis*.

Substitutions Any bergenia would do, for example the white-flowered 'Silberlicht'. In brighter circumstances, you could use softer hostas like 'Frances Williams'. If you find the tovara too vivid, you could replace it with one of the fancy sorts of *Ajuga reptans*, like the purple-leaved 'Atropurpurea', with its spikes of deep blue flowers in early summer.

Ideas for its use This planting could be stretched or replicated for a bigger border in damp shade. Here, stones are set in grass for access, though perhaps an edging of periwinkle (the double blue is good), or even *Helxine solierolii* (though that plant's emerald green carpets can sometimes be a nuisance) would emphasise the design. The planting would also make an attractive central bed, in a rectangle of brick, with outer borders to match from page 130.

Planting 7 Colour all season with rustic simplicity

John Codrington's garden near Rutland Water is crammed with good planting ideas, and is frequently photographed. While some of his lush woodland plantings might be too dense for the smaller garden, simple narrow borders like this are much more common. This planting – seen here in April – offers a charming and informal solution to the problem of how to achieve a sequence of continuous colour with almost no need for constant re-planting.

1 *Tulipa* 'Red Triumphator'
2 *Tulipa* 'Yellow Triumphator'
3 *Milium effusum* 'Bowles Golden'
4 *Sedum spectabile*
5 *Knautia arvensis*
6 *Lunaria annua* deep purple form (honesty)
7 *Lunaria annua* white form (honesty)
8 *Iris* 'Blue Surprise'
9 *Narcissus* 'Mount Hood'
10 *Rosa* 'Etoile d'Hollande'
11 *Clematis macropetala*
12 *Stachys olympica*

ON PLAN ONLY
A *Lavandula* 'Old English' (lavender)
B *Tulipa* 'Queen of the Night'
C *Tulipa* white

Developments and the seasons   To achieve the wild look even earlier in spring, use a scattering of yellow winter aconites or some of the oriental adonises (*Adonis amurensis* is like a large aconite, and some forms have astonishingly frilled and divided leaves). *Leucojum vernum* (snowflake) would register far better here than the commoner snowdrop and could be followed by bluebells. The irises and roses come in for high summer. It would be easy to add later-flowering species clematis like *Clematis macropetala* or *C. orientalis* (there's a good silvery blue one for late summer called *C. x jouiniana* that would look fine against the colour of this stone).

Site   Though there is plenty of sun here, the planting would also do well in partial shade. The tulips would eventually fade away, and need re-planting every few seasons (in this garden, the bulbs are eaten by badgers).

Maintenance and cost   There is nothing very unusual here, and much of it will self-sow. The 'Bowles Golden' grass and honesty need editing ruthlessly. It costs very little to achieve this lovely simple effect: everything can be grown from seed

except the irises (look for 'Cliffs of Dover' in white, and 'Lord Warden' in deep honey yellow), the tulips and the clematis.

Props and additions   This wild looking border needs a patio or courtyard of rustic simplicity, preferably one of rough stones, although crazy paving would do. A few herbs could be added – golden sage, golden marjoram, rosemary, and some pots of mints, basil and so on. 'Eau de Cologne' mint, with its purplish leaves, would look especially good.

Substitutions   The tulips could be changed for other varieties: the lily-flowered types like these are more elegant than the usual 'boxy ones'. Other varieties could be 'Mrs Moon', or those from the group listed in the catalogues as 'viridifloras'.

Ideas for its use   A double depth of this planting would look good, and so would more wall plants. It could then make a pretty square planting around a standard tree, perhaps a variegated holly or a yellow standard rose, or at the base of an arbour. It would also look pretty edging a lawn, backed by a deep green ivied wall, or hedge.

Planting 8 High-speed planting for a sheltered corner

Garden effects can be very quickly achieved: we made this planting as soon as the bulldozers had left, and it is shown here in early July just two seasons old. The low box hedge around the planting was dug from an acquaintance's garden. The only penalty for such dense planting is that it will turn into a jungle after a few more seasons, and will need pulling to pieces – but that is enjoyable too.

Developments and the seasons Clumps of *Narcissus triandrus*, aquilegias and camassias have been planted here for early in the season. Later, there are acid yellow and cream kniphofias ('Percy's Pride' and 'Little Maid'), border penstemons ('Glabra', 'Apple Blossom' and 'Mother of Pearl'), and *Caryopteris clandonensis* for a late haze of soft blue.

1 *Hosta* seedlings
2 *Iris sibirica* 'Alba'
3 *Agapanthus campanulatus* (African lily)
4 *Lilium tigrinum* (tiger lily)
5 *Salvia officinalis* narrow-leaved form (sage)
6 *Acanthus mollis* (bear's breeches)
7 *Helichrysum petiolatum*
8 *Sphaeralcea munroana*
9 *Artemisia* 'Powys Castle'
10 *Thymus drucei* 'Silver Posie' (thyme)
11 *Dianthus* 'Earl of Essex' (pink)
12 *Rosa* 'Tuscany Superb'
13 *Buxus sempervirens* (common box)
14 *Mattueccia struthiopteris* (shuttlecock fern)
15 *Aquilegia* 'Double Pink' (in seed)

ON PLAN ONLY
A *Rosa* 'Mme Isaac Pereire'
B *Rosa* 'The Garland'
C *Lonicera periclymenum* (honeysuckle)
D *Bidens ferulaefolia*
E *Kniphofia* 'Percy's Pride'
F *Geranium pratensis* 'Alba Plena'
G *Hamamelis mollis* 'Pallida'
H *Cardamine pratense* 'Flore Pleno'
I *Rosa spinosissima* 'Double Red'
J *Hosta tokudama* 'Aureo-nebulosa'

1 *Hosta* seedlings
2 *Iris sibirica* 'Alba'
3 *Agapanthus campanulatus* (African lily)
4 *Lilium tigrinum* (tiger lily)
5 *Salvia officinalis* narrow-leaved form (sage)
6 *Acanthus mollis* (bear's breeches)
7 *Helichrysum petiolatum*
8 *Sphaeralcea munroana*
9 *Artemisia* 'Powys Castle'
10 *Thymus drucei* 'Silver Posie' (thyme)
11 *Dianthus* 'Earl of Essex' (pink)
12 *Rosa* 'Tuscany Superb'
13 *Buxus sempervirens* (common box)
14 *Mattueccia struthiopteris* (shuttlecock fern)
15 *Aquilegia* 'Double Pink' (in seed)

Site This planting is in semi-shade, and the plants by the water butt in the corner enjoy only a few hours' sun a day. The overflow from the butt makes the border against that wall damp; perfect for ferns. The *Mattueccia struthiopteris* does especially well, and *Osmunda regalis* would be good too.

Maintenance and cost The main maintenance involves overwintering the pots, especially the tender agapanthus plants, which must not be disturbed: they must be dried off under cover (in a garage, for example) until new leaves appear in spring. The helichrysum will survive a mild winter. In the border, the artemisia can swamp everything nearby, and needs watching and staking, as do the aquilegias (gone over in the picture). The box, too young here to trim, will later on need cutting twice a year.

Props and additions A painted wooden seat makes a pleasant focal point in the right colour. Most modern paints can look brash among plants and must be chosen carefully. Shades of soft green, grey and blue, and even Indian or Chinese red, look far better than raw white. It may be best to mix your own, and 'grey' down any colour you think might jar – this seat has since been repainted slate-grey, which we prefer.

Substitutions The helichrysum in the pot could be replaced with any other silver foliage, such as *Helichrysum microphyllum*. Instead of the agapanthus by the seat, another 'architectural' plant would give a similar effect: well-fed hostas, or eucomis (the pineapple lily) – easy from seed, and often with excellently shaped and coloured foliage. The agapanthus flower stalks here make getting into the seat difficult later in the season. For something perfumed instead of the dianthus, there are plenty of other pinks to choose from, even the garden centre 'Doris', which is longer flowering but has less fragrance.

Ideas for its use This planting is backed, out of the picture, by old cordon apples against the wall, but would look equally fine in front of a rose-covered wall or trellis (perhaps 'Sanders White', mixed with the coral 'Mme Grégoire Staechelin' or the luscious deep pink 'Mme Isaac Pereire' mixed with the Jekyll rose called 'The Garland', in palest amethyst pink).

Planting 9 Luxuriant, golden harmony in shade

This lavish and complicated planting – seen here in August – is one that any plant buff might envy for the plants alone; they are assembled with a wonderful eye for luxuriant harmony. Though it is only a part of the display gardens at Stone House Cottage near Kidderminster (the rest is equally exciting), this section would be perfect for a small shady garden – a constant source of delight.

Developments and the seasons For more autumn colour, you could add the wonderful variegated lacecap hydrangea, and perhaps a dwarf hosta like *Hosta lancifolia* (for amethyst flowers). The trees planted to give shade could be koelreuteria, ailanthus or even a yellow-fruited malus (crab apple) like 'Yellow Siberian' (though none with purple leaves), and not the yellow robinia, which is too brilliant. The hellebores and pulmonarias flower in spring, and the fuchsias, hydrangeas and hostas will go on until early autumn. If you'd die without some bulbs, keep them to pots or tubs.

Site Moderate shade suits this planting well, and it would do excellently beneath existing trees or large shrubs. In fact, strong sunlight often damages the yellow-foliaged plants that give this planting its harmony.

Maintenance and cost Once the basic plant cost is borne, there is little else. Feed to ensure the hosta and geraniums give their best. Otherwise, remove finished seed heads from the hellebores (unless you want the seed) and spent flower stalks from the geraniums, and lightly prune the hydrangeas.

Props and additions Silvery natural wood for seating and tubs, and green crusted terracotta for pots would look appropriate here. Pots might have double shell-pink tulips for spring, yellow or maroon lilies for summer, or perhaps (if it is sunny enough) a white or yellow *Argyranthemum frutescens* (like 'Jamaica Primrose'). Even a big potful of aspidistra would look attractive, if you wanted to put it outdoors for the summer. To add more fragrance, you could put a few pots of pale

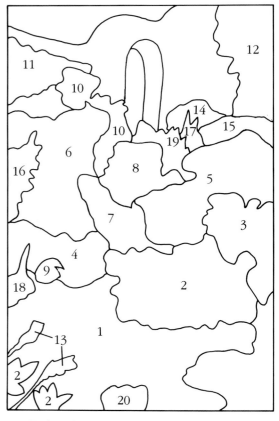

1 *Fuchsia* 'Genii'
2 *Helleborus orientalis* 'Black Knight' seedlings (lenten rose)
3 *Hosta sieboldiana*
4 *Geranium clarkei* 'Kashmir White'
5 *Viburnum opulus* 'Luteus' (guelder rose)
6 *Viburnum tinus* 'Variegatum' (laurustinus)
7 *Anemone hupehensis* (Japanese anemone)
8 *Hydrangea serrata* 'Rosalba'
9 *Iris pseudacorus* 'Variegata'
10 *Rubus ulmifolius* 'Variegata'
11 *Jasminum stephanense* (jasmine)
12 *Clematis* 'Marjorie'
13 *Heuchera* 'Greenfinch' (coral flower)
14 *Ribes* 'Brocklebankii' (flowering currant)
15 *Cornus mas* 'Elegantissima' (dogwood)
16 *Campanula patula*
17 *Astilbe* sp.
18 *Pulmonaria saccharata* 'Greenmantle' (lungwort)
19 *Iris pseudacorus* 'Bastardii'
20 *Geranium macrorhizum* 'Variegatum'

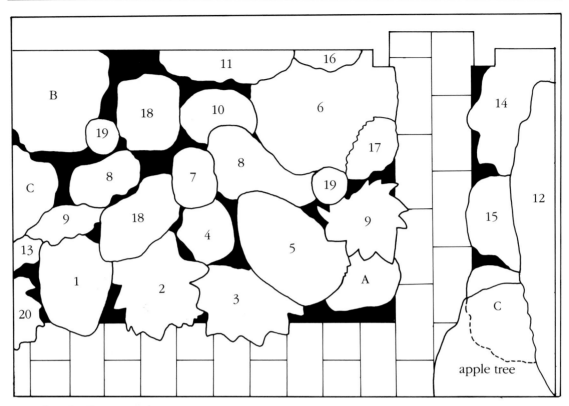

1 *Fuchsia* 'Genii'
2 *Helleborus orientalis* 'Black Knight' seedlings (lenten rose)
3 *Hosta sieboldiana*
4 *Geranium clarkei* 'Kashmir White'
5 *Viburnum opulus* 'Luteus' (guelder rose)
6 *Viburnum tinus* 'Variegatum' (laurustinus)
7 *Anemone hupehensis* (Japanese anemone)
8 *Hydrangea serrata* 'Rosalba'
9 *Iris pseudacorus* 'Variegata'
10 *Rubus ulmifolius* 'Variegata'
11 *Jasminum stephanense* (jasmine)
12 *Clematis* 'Marjorie'
13 *Heuchera* 'Greenfinch' (coral flower)
14 *Ribes* 'Brocklebankii' (flowering currant)
15 *Cornus mas* 'Elegantissima' (dogwood)
16 *Campanula patula*
17 *Astilbe* sp.
18 *Pulmonaria saccharata* 'Greenmantle' (lungwort)
19 *Iris pseudacorus* 'Bastardii'
20 *Geranium macrorhizum* 'Variegatum'

ON PLAN ONLY
A *Tiarella polyphylla*
B *Hydrangea* 'Prezioza'
C *Romneya coulteri*

pink stocks by the seat (surprisingly, the heuchera has an excellent perfume).

Substitutions   This handsome and serene planting is fairly easily recreated. The rubus might be difficult to find, and it does not always grow as vigorously as here. There is nothing more common that could easily take its place, so you could perhaps add another silver variegated dogwood. For the wall climbers and shrubs, *Clematis viticella* 'Plena' would also be good, or even 'Kermesina' if you want something showier (the large-flowered hybrids would look out of place here). The dangling winter catkins of *Garrya elliptica*, or the more glamorous summer ones of *Itea illicifolia* (see page 136) would look good against the wall in place of the clematis.

Ideas for its use   The soft yellowish green tonality, and the restraint of the planting, suit it more to paving or gravel than to the bright green of grass. It would also make a stunning front garden, or a border beneath a row of collector's trees.

Planting 10 Refined formality in soft yellows

While there are plenty of easily maintained hard surfaces in this garden, The Priory at Kemerton, how much more stylish it is than the usual concrete and raised beds (and not a great deal more expensive). The planting, seen here in late summer, has a refined colour scheme based on shades of soft yellow, with touches of purple and grey-blue – and cream and violet together in the extraordinary and beautiful clematis (*Clematis florida* 'Sieboldii') on

ON PLAN ONLY
A *Cheiranthus* 'Harpur Crewe'
B *Hemerocallis* 'lemon'
C *Kniphofia* 'Goldelse'
D *Waldsteinia ternata*
E *Anthemis cupaniana*
F *Bidens ferulaefolia*
G *Ranunculus ficaria* 'Anemone flowered'
H Standard golden box

1 *Dahlia*, 'Coltness' yellow form
2 *Lavandula* 'Old English' (lavender)
3 *Alchemilla mollis* (lady's mantle)
4 *Helichrysum angustifolium* (curry plant)
5 *Echeveria* sp.
6 *Passiflora racemosa* seedling
7 *Clematis florida* 'Sieboldii'
8 *Actinidia kolomitka*
9 *Datura* 'Grand Marnier'
10 *Citrus limon* (lemon)
11 *Jasminum officinale* (common white jasmine)
12 *Fuchsia* species
13 *Hieracium* sp.
14 *Lilium* 'Connecticut King'
15 *Lilium* 'Pink Perfection'
16 *Lilium speciosum*
17 *Buxus sempervirens* (common box)
18 Box, corner left unpruned
19 Cherry
20 Apple
21 Hawthorn
22 *Thymus x citriodorus* 'Aureus'
23 *Argyranthemum* 'Vancouver'

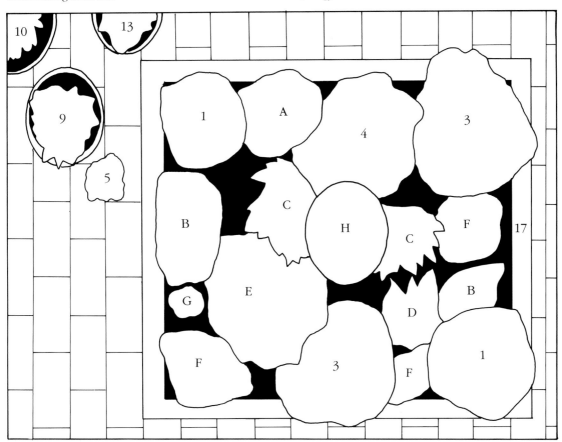

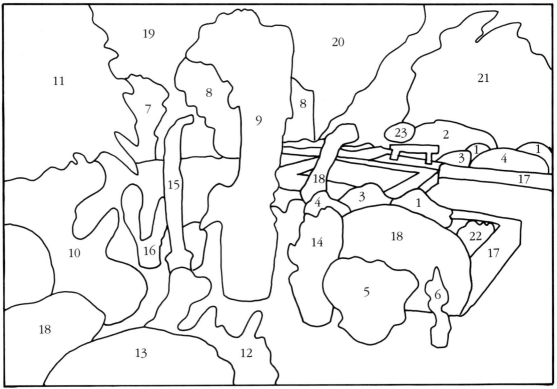

the back wall. Plants in pots are an essential part of this look, and the emphasis is on rather exotic and tender things like lemons and the magnificent datura.

Developments and the seasons   Here, artifice is all. In spring, pack the beds with soft yellow daffodils (some of the 'triandrus' hybrids would be especially good), and let the alchemilla cover the dying leaves. Walls or fences could usefully have a mix of white and yellow roses. One side of this garden is taken up by a roofed shelter; the roof, if you built something similar, could be swathed in jasmine and the glossy-leaved yellow rose 'Gold-finch', which both have a marvellous scent.

Site   The silver-leaved plants need the sunniest wall; otherwise, most things here will succeed in moderate shade. This courtyard must also be very sheltered; the smaller pots would topple over in windy conditions.

1 *Dahlia*, 'Coltness' yellow form
2 *Lavandula* 'Old English' (lavender)
3 *Alchemilla mollis* (lady's mantle)
4 *Helichrysum angustifolium* (curry plant)
5 *Echeveria* sp.
6 *Passiflora racemosa* seedling
7 *Clematis florida* 'Sieboldii'
8 *Actinidia kolomitka*
9 *Datura* 'Grand Marnier'
10 *Citrus limon* (lemon)
11 *Jasminum officinale* (common white jasmine)
12 *Fuchsia* species
13 *Hieracium* sp.
14 *Lilium* 'Connecticut King'
15 *Lilium* 'Pink Perfection'
16 *Lilium speciosum*
17 *Buxus sempervirens* (common box)
18 Box, corner left unpruned
19 Cherry
20 Apple
21 Hawthorn
22 *Thymus x citriodorus* 'Aureus'
23 *Argyranthemum* 'Vancouver'

Maintenance and cost   Maintenance consists largely of keeping the alchemilla from swamping everything else, and trimming the box (it could be left to grow a little larger than it is here). Every second season in small box-edged beds like these, it's worth slicing downwards with a spade on the inside of the plants, to stop the box roots draining all nourishment from the flowers. Keep the flowers well fed for a good show. The main cost is in the hard surfaces; plant costs are comparatively small. It might be possible to buy large daturas if you live in London; otherwise they will have to be grown from seed.

Props and additions   Simple terracotta pots and wooden tubs are used here, but oriental glazed pots would also look good. White-painted furniture would be rather dominating: natural wood painted deep slate grey, soft yellow, or even Chinese red would be better. Other plants to grow in pots might include a few large specimens of *Bidens ferulae-folia*, the marvellous golden *Cassia corymbosa*, and the filigree-leaved *Chrysanthemum mawii*. A few pots on the rim of the pool would be worth having (fill with *Francoa ramosa*).

Substitutions   This charming planting, young yet, uses mostly simple plants in simple colours, in a strongly architectural framework of square beds and square pool. In the beds, almost any mix of the listed plants, or others in the same shades, would be good. The daturas could also be white, as in *Datura suaveolens*, instead of the yellow sort, as here.

Ideas for its use   This would make a perfect courtyard or patio where minimal upkeep is required, and where the tender pot plants can be overwintered.

Planting 11 Exotica for high summer

This sumptuous colour scheme of greys, pinks, purples, and light blue at Great Dixter in Sussex – photographed in late July – has been worked out mostly in bold and architectural foliage. It is an exciting and glamorous way of handling a small sunny space such as a patio. Good plant form and carefully chosen colours can be infinitely more satisfying than the usual potted conifer, scarlet pelargoniums and bedding plants, and are just as easy to do.

Developments and the seasons   This planting will be at its best from about mid-June until September, but if you have no other garden and need early colour, bring in some potted bulbs (there are plenty of varieties of tulip to match this colour scheme). It would be fun to twine the back of the planting with a purple clematis, perhaps the deep purple 'Kermesse' or any of the lovely

Clematis alpina variants. A lavender-blue catmint like 'Six Hills', and some white-flowering bergenias (try 'Silberlicht') could be added low down at the front, along with some irises. The pink *Potentilla nepalensis* 'Miss Willmott' might also be a nice addition for high summer.

Site   This planting needs a good amount of light, warmth and sun, but will succeed even on poorish soil. Feeding would help the cardoon foliage, but it is not essential. Try to have a sheltered site: canna flowers and leaves are easily damaged, although everything else is wind- and weather-proof.

Maintenance and cost   The main problem with this lush sort of planting is in overwintering the tender species. The verbena, salvia and canna are only half-hardy – hard frost will kill them – but the

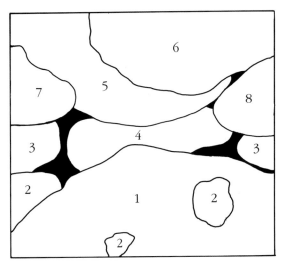

1 *Verbena* 'Silver Anne'
2 *Salvia patens* 'Cambridge Blue'
3 *Monarda* 'Croftway Scarlet' (sweet bergamot)
4 *Canna* purple-leaved form
5 *Cynara cardunculus* (cardoon)
6 *Rosa* 'Moyesii' (species rose)
7 *Phlox paniculata* 'Brigadier'
8 *Phlox paniculata* 'Alba'

verbena may be overwintered as cuttings (they root very easily) or raised from seed in mixed colours, though you would need to start early in the season. Salvia roots can be dug up just like ordinary dahlias, and overwintered in a box of dry peat in a cold frame, shed or garage. It also seeds plentifully, and you can easily collect some in late September. The canna also needs lifting and overwintering in a box of dry peat (use the same one for the salvia roots). Otherwise, maintenance is easy. As the cardoon comes into flower (you will see a substantial stem arising from the rosette of jagged silvery leaves), cut it out: the flower stems grow vast, flower dully, and usually blow over untidily.

Props and additions   This could be a good background for an assortment of pots and tubs. Pelargoniums in white and deep plum, or some of the fancy-leaved types (such as 'Crocodile', and the lovely 'Mrs Quilter' with golden-yellow leaves), would look good with other verbenas and some of the half-hardy osteospermums, especially the wonderful 'Blue Streak'.

Substitutions   The wonderful salvia is more easily found, and will look just as good, in its equally thrilling mid-blue form. The monarda is easy to find, and other interesting colours are also easily raised from seed. Artichokes would do instead of the cardoon, although the leaves are a little less glamorous. Cardoons have smaller flower-heads (too small to eat), though their leaf mid-ribs are edible.

Ideas for its use   Besides being suitable for a hot patio, this planting could be used wherever there is a need for a good general planting for high and late summer.

Country Mixes

The idea of a country garden has such a strong appeal for all town-dwellers, and is so prominent in advertising and the media that it seems almost to have a concrete existence. However, looking at gardens in the real countryside does not reveal any clear style of gardening: bright red gravel and blue lobelias are quite as common as old roses and faded delphiniums; and even garden layouts are immensely variable. It is sometimes suggested that formal gardens are most suitable for 'town' (whatever that is) and the informal, rambling, chintzy, look for the countryside, but such divisions are unjustified: it is possible to find exquisitely formal gardens (which might seem urban) surrounding Regency bungalows in wildest Dorset, as well as tangles of fruit trees, rare weeds and *Alchemilla mollis* burgeoning just off London's Eaton Square. Neither looks in the least out of place; they just happen to suit the taste of the owner.

There is, however, a particular mix of shrubs, herbaceous plants and annuals (and in grand examples, half-hardy plants planted out in spring as large specimens) that often look wonderful in the country, and are more often to be found there. This way of planting allows for an exciting range of plants to be included, though this freedom does occasionally present difficulties. Plantings that seem to fit the 'country style' are grouped here, but if inner city or suburban gardeners like them, there is no reason why they cannot grow them too.

One factor important in real country gardens is that land is usually a lot cheaper in the countryside than near a city, so gardens are often bigger. They may allow for the full panoply of herbaceous borders, rose gardens, herb and vegetable gardens, orchards and tennis courts, or at least a few apple and pear trees, a lawn and a flower bed with a seat beside it. They also allow the gardener to grow biennial plants like foxgloves out of sight for their first season, and then to move them to their flowering positions in the second season. This happens in several gardens here. If you have only a cottage-sized plot, and a proper cottage (not the sort with ten bedrooms), your garden would look lovely either with some sort of variation of the planting on page 52 or with the traditional cottage-garden mix of old roses, simple flowers, and 'fruit and veg'. If you really want to emulate the designers' 'country look' in this chapter, avoid heathers, Lawson's cypress, dwarf conifers, begonias, and brash roses like 'Masquerade' (though you might well find that the gardens of real villagers will be crammed with just such things).

Pear and apple trees are essential in a country garden (and lovely), and should, ideally, be grown as standards, not on dwarfing stock (and do not need much pruning). Cherries are wonderful in flower, and some pear varieties (such as 'Catillac') can easily match them. If you have room, plant plums and damsons too, or try less familiar crops like medlars, myrobalans (the earliest fruit crop of all to flower – and almond scented), bullaces and filberts. Up-market props such as architectural trellis work, grand statuary and urns, will probably look out of place; plank seats and simple containers are all that are necessary. Keep the plan formal:

island beds do not look right and should be avoided, along with the associated hanging-baskets and fake hay baskets filled with petunias.

The larger your garden the more elements may be added: perhaps a proper cut lawn and herbaceous borders, a rose garden, and some decent hedges. Alternatively, you could try a mix of orchard and woodland garden around a wildish lawn – not the sort to be decorated with floral loungers or 'patio sets' – and a section of one of these 'country mix' plantings. A ramshackle garden house beside an equally ramshackle barbeque might be a nice addition, perhaps next to the salad and herb garden (see page 148); barbeque smoke, and the cooked results, are vastly improved by burning a few twigs of oregano, savory or rosemary, and served with a salad just harvested from nearby.

Another essential element of a country garden is roses. There are many ways of including them, either in mixed plantings or in rose gardens or 'rosariums'. Though modern roses are often used skilfully (there is a marvellous planting in yellow and white in what used to be the private garden at Tyninghame in East Lothian), the usual assemblage of 'Peace', 'Whisky Mac' and whatever is named after the latest royal event, can look dull. For the same reason, avoid using hybrid tea roses as large perennial bedding plants, which are often seen with polyantha in rose gardens where nothing else grows. It is more appropriate in a country garden, and less work, to have either old roses or species roses as full-sized shrubs, letting them grow without any pruning, and simply working them into the rest of the garden. Even hybrid teas can sometimes look good treated in this way, and do not pose the

risk of losing every flower if it rains at the wrong time as do the old varieties, though the show and perfume of the old types can be stunning if the season works properly.

If you want a proper rosarium, then either use some of the lovely smaller species roses and varieties, or be prepared to keep bigger ones under control. Roses (old and new) often also need a good formal design idea to make them look their best: they can look untidy left to themselves (it is part of their charm). Neat box edges, or a parterre of grass paths around them, look good. Some of the best varieties (such as 'Fantin Latour', 'Ispahan' and 'Ville de Bruxelles') need some support, perhaps a couple of horizontal stakes supported 60–100 cm (2–3 ft) off the ground, so that the plants' stems can flop over without being too near the ground.

Another feature of the 'country look' is to grow climbing roses into your old apple tree if you have them (as at Sissinghurst, and so on). This, though inconvenient when the trees eventually fall beneath the weight of flowers, can look wonderful, using varieties of rose like 'Paul's Himalayan Musk', 'Bobbie James', 'Seagull', 'Mme Alfred Carrière' or even the old rose 'Alba Plena' (which looks extremely fine climbing into an ancient laburnum). All of them need planting at least 1 m (3 ft) away from the trunk of whatever tree you plan to swamp. A slanting pole should then be placed from the rose into the crown of the tree. The roses shown in these pages have been integrated thoroughly into the garden itself, from the lovely half-hedge of the ancient 'Rosa Mundi' on page 62, to the sheet of modern 'Felicia' (which also makes excellent standards) on page 57.

Planting 12 A rustic abundance with self-sown plants

This is the street boundary of the garden at Crossing House in Cambridgeshire, photographed in July. It seems a perfect way of planting along a simple piece of fencing to give both owner and the outside world vast pleasure, and without risking more treasured plants. Many of these seed themselves or are otherwise fairly persistent, so a certain amount of footballing and dog trampling will not destroy the design.

Developments and the seasons The delicacy of most of the plants in this small-scale border contrasts with the solid lines of the fence and the powerful clump of lily. For early spring, a small crocus, perhaps *Crocus sieberi*, in white with a glowing orange style, and certainly plenty of pale gold and honey-scented *C. susianus*, could be planted, and followed by small tulips, especially *Tulipa clusiana* (the lady tulip) and the starry *T. turkestanica* (which persists quite well). If you couldn't live without daffs, then one of the charming cyclamineus hybrids such as 'Jack Snipe' or 'Tête à Tête' would be perfect. Then the planting itself takes over, with something in flower for most of the season. If you have a suitable location nearby, plant the autumn-flowering *Clematis flammula*, almost like the wild 'old man's beard', rampant, and with a rather more carrying (and ravishing) perfume.

Site This planting is south-east facing, with sun in the morning and shade thereafter. It would do anywhere with moderate sun.

1 *Iberis amara* (candytuft)
2 *Calendula officinalis* (pot marigold)
3 *Potentilla nepalensis* cultivar (cinquefoil)
4 *Delphinium consolida* (larkspur)
5 *Mimulus moschatus* (monkey musk)
6 *Papaver rupifragum*
7 *Helleborus orientalis* (lenten rose)
8 *Rosa* 'Amy Robsart'
9 *Viola odorata* (sweet violet)
10 *Hedera helix* (common ivy)
11 *Nepeta* 'Six Hills' (catmint)
12 *Lilium tigrinum* 'Pink Beauty' (tiger lily)
13 *Dianthus* double soft pink form (pink)
14 *Aubrietia* seed grown
15 *Agapanthus umbellatus* navy blue form (African lily)
16 *Digitalis purpurea* (foxglove)

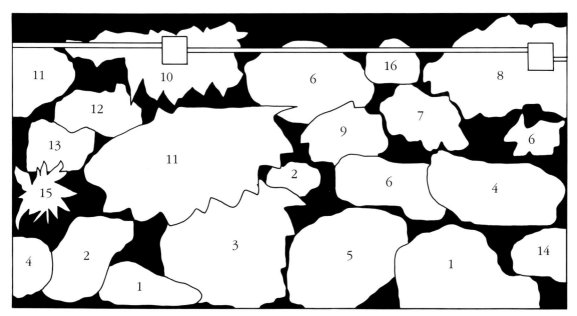

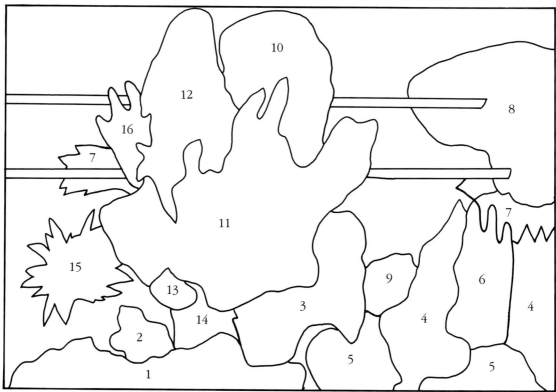

Maintenance and cost Almost nothing here costs more than the price of a packet of seeds. Even the agapanthus could be seed grown. The rose and the lily will cost a few pounds to buy. In subsequent seasons you will have to remove excess self-grown seedlings. The foxglove is biennial, and you will need to sow in two consecutive seasons to have flowers every season thereafter.

Props and additions Here, rusticity is all (even though the garden inside the fence is packed with rarities and a number of grand props). Seats made of planking, pots of recycled bits and pieces, with interesting geraniums, 'Lass of Gowrie' or 'Crystal Palace Gem'. Good roses for it would be the lovely 'Blush Noisette', and the old Scots white (*Rosa spinosissima*), if you stop it running and don't mind its short but delicious season. You could also add some sweet violet cultivars ('Rosina' would be especially apt, and perhaps the pure white).

Substitutions This lovely tangle, planted on the street side verge of the house, is not as easy to find substitutions for as a quick glance might suggest. None of the plants are difficult to find, and everything is easy to grow. Much of it will happily self-sow so the precise look will change from year to year. If you dislike the hot orange marigolds, replace them with some of the paler 'Art Shades', often lemon and lovely, or the bronze 'Neon'. An equally easy lily would be *Lilium regale*.

Ideas for its use This would also make a good boundary planting against a paddock or an orchard margin, or even the next-door garden. It could also be used to divide the kitchen garden from the lawn.

1 *Iberis amara* (candytuft)
2 *Calendula officinalis* (pot marigold)
3 *Potentilla nepalensis* cultivar (cinquefoil)
4 *Delphinium consolida* (larkspur)
5 *Mimulus moschatus* (monkey musk)
6 *Papaver rupifragum*
7 *Helleborus orientalis* (lenten rose)
8 *Rosa* 'Amy Robsart'
9 *Viola odorata* (sweet violet)
10 *Hedera helix* (common ivy)
11 *Nepeta* 'Six Hills' (catmint)
12 *Lilium tigrinum* 'Pink Beauty' (tiger lily)
13 *Dianthus* double soft pink form (pink)
14 *Aubrietia* seed grown
15 *Agapanthus umbellatus* navy blue form (African lily)
16 *Digitalis purpurea* (foxglove)

Planting 13 Close harmonies for light shade

This is another planting from the rich vein of planting at Great Dixter in Sussex. It is a developed harmony from the blue-grey leaves and amber-red stems of the pretty rose bush (fast growing, and easy from seed, too, if you can find it). The soft pinks and blues of the flowers team well with the purple perilla leaves and are sharpened up by the foliage of the variegated grass.

Developments and the seasons   This planting starts in late June with the delightful rose and will keep going well into the autumn. For an earlier start, the addition of a good pulmonaria like 'Redstart' would harmonise well: it has lovely brick-pink flowers from February or so. For colour from March to May you could plant auriculas, possibly in pale blue (look especially for one called 'Mrs Cairns' Blue'), and shades of tan and pale yellow (which usually have the best smell). If you want spring bulbs, add the ones described on page 30.

Site   Half shade would be fine for this planting, and moist soil would help, though none of the plants are especially fussy. Avoid a dry south-facing border.

Maintenance and cost   The perilla is not always easy to find, so could (just) be omitted. The grass needs to be kept under rigorous control, so cut it back whenever it gets too high or too wide. It will soon re-sprout. Prune the hydrangeas in the same way as any of the less grand mopheads.

Props and additions   You could add pots of white lilies – *Lilium imperiale* or *L. formosanum* – carefully staked, and which have flowering stems for much of the season, and possibly some potted hostas, or even *Francoa sonchifolia* or the rather better but rarer *F. ramosa*, both of whose

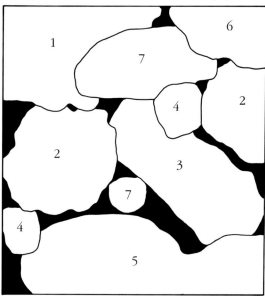

1 *Rosa glauca* (shrub rose)
2 *Hydrangea* 'Générale Vicomtesse de Vibraye'
3 *Astilbe taquetii*
4 *Perilla* purple-leaved form
5 *Phalaris arundinacea* (gardener's garters grass)
6 *Eucryphia x intermedia*
7 *Lychnis coronaria* (campion)

pinkish flowers would work perfectly here at the height of the season.

Substitutions The big blobs of the china blue mophead hydrangeas could easily be replaced by the slightly more refined circlets of some of the lacecap hydrangeas, perhaps the usual though lovely 'Blue Wave'. There are a number of pink astilbes to choose from. The grass, the formidable 'gardener's garters', would be too invasive for such a refined planting in a smaller space; substitute variegated *Arrhenatherum bulbosum* (which looks slightly bluer). The rose is the only one available

with such subtle leaf colour; the flowers are soft pink, paler in the centre, and single; the hips are a violent orange red. If you can't find the right purple-leaved perilla from seed, try a purple-leaved heliotrope, or use the dark-leaved basil called 'Opal' (if you garden somewhere warm).

Ideas for its use This would also make a good forecourt garden for a town house, or for the shady parts of a small backyard, where you could add plenty of ferns, and even a hosta or two – perhaps appending the planting on page 24.

Planting 14 Sophisticated tangle in a formal layout

This lush planting is part of a sophisticated Dorset garden where stylish formal layout and clever colour schemes are allied to interesting plants. Though surrounding what might be called a cottage, the garden is on the fringes of an eighteenth-century landscaped park, and loses nothing by the contrast. The owner had, until recently, a garden in France and this has perhaps been a source of inspiration for the colour and design of this garden; the luxuriant herbaceous plantings work wonderfully within the framework of box hedges and rows of topiary box domes.

Developments and the seasons The planting will be in full fig from high summer until late autumn (when the caryopteris and ceratostigmas will still be producing blue flowers to make up for grey autumn skies). For spring, keep the silver

and pinky-blue scheme going with the little bulb *Ipheion* 'Wisley Blue', with its soft blue stars, and perhaps an ornithogalum like the delectable *Ornithogalum nutans*.

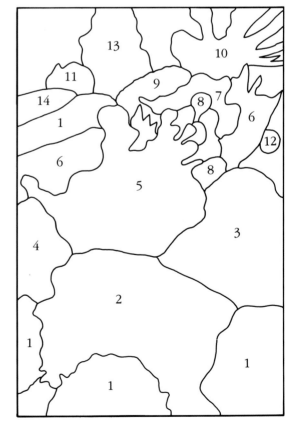

 1 *Buxus sempervirens* (common box)
 2 *Heuchera* 'Palace Purple' (coral flower)
 3 *Salvia patens* 'Cambridge Blue'
 4 *Ceratostigma willmottianum*
 5 *Achillea* 'Gold Plate'
 6 *Artemisia* 'Powys Castle'
 7 *Perovskia atriplicifolia*
 8 *Allium christophii* (seedheads)
 9 *Caryopteris clandonensis*
10 *Onopordum acanthium* (Scotch thistle)
11 *Agapanthus* Headbourne hybrids (African lily)
12 *Osteospermum juncundum* 'Langtrees'
13 *Ilex aquifolium* (holly)
14 *Lavandula* 'Hidcote' (lavender)

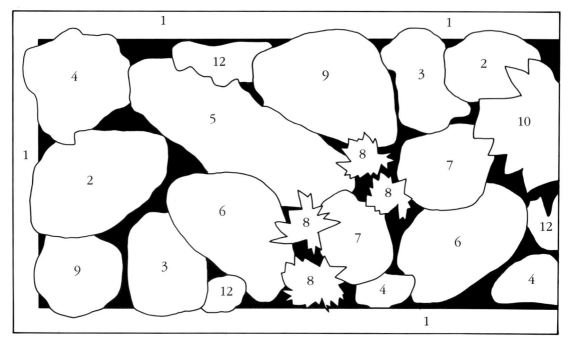

1 *Buxus sempervirens* (common box)
2 *Heuchera* 'Palace Purple' (coral flower)
3 *Salvia patens* 'Cambridge Blue'
4 *Ceratostigma willmottianum*
5 *Achillea* 'Gold Plate'
6 *Artemisia* 'Powys Castle'
7 *Perovskia atriplicifolia*

8 *Allium christophii* (seedheads)
9 *Caryopteris clandonensis*
10 *Onopordum acanthium* (Scotch thistle)
11 *Agapanthus* Headbourne hybrids (African lily)
12 *Osteospermum juncundum* 'Langtrees'
13 *Ilex aquifolium* (holly)
14 *Lavandula* 'Hidcote' (lavender)

Site This border is on the south side of the house, in full sun, though the plants here would cope with some shade. It faces a yew-fringed lawn.

Maintenance and cost This border does need regular maintenance (see page 8) – being mostly herbaceous material – and this will include trimming the artemisias when flowering is over (or before if you just want silvery foliage), and dead-heading the achilleas. Dig up the salvia roots in the autumn, and overwinter as for a dahlia – or save plenty of seed, and start it off under glass early the next spring.

Props and additions Such a sophisticated planting could cope with almost any sort of prop, from plank seats to things much grander. The garden here has both splendid pots and lead tanks and tubs of heliotropes (a wonderful almond scent on warm days), big pots of the exotic-looking, though easy,

pineapple lilies (*Eucomis bicolor* especially) and white agapanthus. To be really grand, a double white datura (or *Datura suaveolens* from seed) would suit this planting. The garden also has some pots of the elegantly dangling and jade-green flowered *Galtonia princeps* (summer hyacinth).

Substitutions Everything here is easy to find, except perhaps for the salvia (some seed merchants now sell it). You might prefer a full edging of box, or dense mounds of the silver *Santolina chamaecyparissus* for even more style. The ochre of the achillea could be changed for a sharper yellow if you prefer. The only plant unsuited to a small garden is the spiny Scotch thistle (*Onopordum*) which is fine when small with its scalloped silver leaves, but thereafter it's vast and tends to fall over in a wind. Being very spiny indeed, that's a major nuisance. In small spaces, use *Erigeron philadelphicus* instead.

Ideas for its use This would make an attractive border round a brick paved yard, or beside a path to a front door. It would associate wonderfully with silver-leaved trees, perhaps the usual pear (*Pyrus* salicifolia)*, or better, if you've more space, the wonderful silver willow (*Salix alba* 'Argentea'). The border would also look good beneath gnarled apple trees.

Planting 15 Country charm in a 'hedgerow' border

In this lovely fragment of a Scottish plantsman's garden in Glenfarg, near Perth, the euphorbia is the only plant that is not easy to find. Most of the others can even be grown from seed with no trouble (sow nos. 3, 6 and 7 in the autumn in pots outdoors, so that they freeze). This lovely combination of plants, seen here in late June, is redolent of the countryside.

Developments and the seasons Much of the planting is fully herbaceous and dies to the ground in winter, offering a perfect opportunity for a good spring planting of bulbs. Add the March- and April-flowering yellow-green hellebore (*H. corsicus*), and plenty pale yellow daffodils, yellow and green tulips, and a few soft pink ones. The euphorbias and the viola will engulf the bulb leaves once the flowers are finished. The eryngiums will give handsome architectural flower stems until autumn. The yellow verbascum will be in flower after most of the foxgloves have finished, so its brightness will not distract the eye from their softer colours.

Site The border is only slightly shaded, but is quite far north (just south of Perth), so would happily take more shade in the south.

Maintenance and cost Maintenance is simple: cut back the foxgloves once they're more or less over, and save a few seed pods. Do the same for the verbascum. The viola might need roughly cutting back if it grows too big for its space. The myrrhis, young here, will eventually produce a wonderful mass of ferny leaves, and tall stems with white carrot flowers. Thereafter, the black seed pods, smelling of anise, will glitter handsomely until they fall (save a few, but cut the stalks before too many fall to the soil). Most of the plants can be grown for a pound or two from seed; only the eryngium will cost more than that.

Props and additions Charming rustic plantings like this need simple pots of ginger mint, soft pink geraniums, ferns, or even stock and a dianthus like 'Loveliness'. All reflect the strong 'country' feel of the plant mix.

Substitutions This pretty and informal planting is easily put together. If you prefer, try the ordinary white form of the common foxglove instead of this large variety (or a mixture of the two). Since they are biennials, you need to have plants coming on to flower next season, either in the border here or elsewhere. These will die out at the end of the year. If you want something perennial, try the gorgeous *D. x mertonensis* (easy from seed), which lives for several years if you keep it well fed. The flowers are a wonderful crushed-strawberry pink. The viola, here in a fancy form, would be as lovely in the pure species, or even as 'Julian', a sharp violet-blue. The eryngium has well-veined leaves, though you might prefer the clusters of steely blue flower heads of a species like *Eryngium alpinum*, or the slightly smaller *E. planum*. The silver foliage of the verbascum is good, and pink-flowered cultivars like 'Pink Domino', which could be used here, have less handsome leaves.

Ideas for its use This would look good in an informal, overgrown garden, perhaps round a circular lawn, with a few apple or cherry trees.

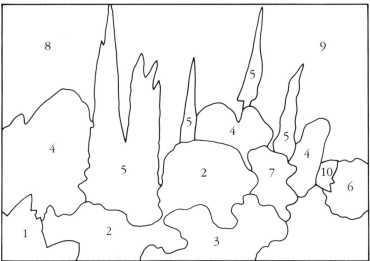

1 *Verbascum olympium* (mullein)
2 *Viola cornuta*
3 *Eryngium tripartitum*
4 *Euphorbia* sp.
5 *Digitalis* 'Excelsior' hybrids (foxglove)
6 *Lilium martagon*
7 *Myrrhis odorata*
8 *Hedera helix* (common ivy)
9 Apple on tunnel frame
10 *Lunaria annua* 'Variegata' (honesty)

Planting 16 Roses and pinks for summer fragrance

On a warm summer morning, with the promise of heat shimmering in the sky, this garden is filled with the intoxicating smell of roses and the spicy sweetness of the extraordinary dianthus (the petals are but fringes of gorgeously coloured threads). Even late into autumn, 'Ballerina' will still be heavy with flowers, and the pear will change from silver to gold.

Developments and the seasons This sumptuous planting will be in flower from earliest June onwards. For earlier in the season, you might like to have pulmonarias ('Sissinghurst White' or 'Cambridge Blue' would be good choices) under the 'Ballerinas', and perhaps some clumps of the starry-flowered *Camassia leichtlinii* and a pale blue iris like 'Harbour Blue', or 'Aline' (which has a stronger, and ravishing, smell).

Site This planting is in an open and sunny courtyard. You will need something similar for the dianthus to do well, though the roses and the foxgloves can take more shade.

Maintenance and cost Only the roses and the pear tree are expensive. The foxgloves are cheap and biennial, and need replacing each season. They will seed themselves, if you let them. (You could plant *Digitalis x mertonensis* instead, as it is reasonably perennial.) For cultivation of the dianthus, see the note on page 119. The roses will not need any pruning until they become impenetrable. 'Ballerina' is prone to blackspot, so you may need to do some spraying. The dying flower sprays of the catmint can be cut right out two or three times a summer, to let new growth through. Plants are easily divided in autumn if you need more.

1 *Chrysanthemum parthenium* (feverfew)
2 *Nepeta* 'Six Hills' (catmint)
3 *Dianthus* 'Rainbow Loveliness' (pink)
4 *Rosa* 'Ballerina'

5 *Rosa* 'Felicia'
6 *Digitalis* 'Excelsior' (foxglove)
7 *Pyrus salicifolia* (silver-leaved pear)

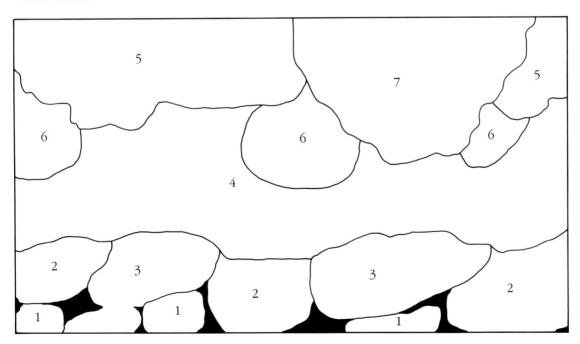

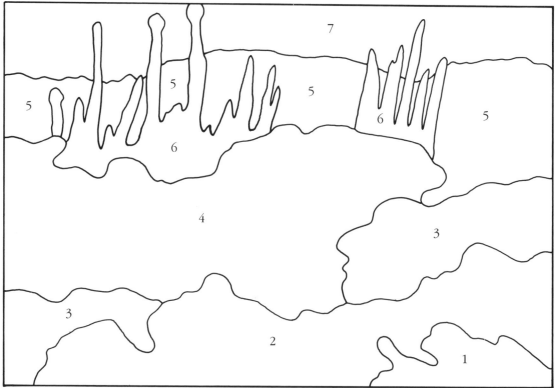

Props and additions For a planting as luscious and sweet as this, any pots for adjacent paving could be planted as on page 68, or page 71 if the geraniums were pale pink. The seating in this garden is Victorian and rustic, but painted fake Lutyens would do; it could even be white.

Substitutions 'Ballerina' is an excellent, hardy and elegant rose, flowering all season, but unperfumed. The lack of perfume is more than made up by the other rose and the dianthus, which will scent the entire garden. For the foxglove, an old form called 'Sutton's Apricot' would look equally good, though the ordinary wild one, or its white form, would be lovely too. The other rose instead of the lovely and perfumed 'Felicia' used here could easily be the climber 'Mme Grégoire Staechelin' on a low trellis, or even 'New Dawn'. I'd hunt, though, for the enchanting 'Stanwell Perpetual', a hybrid with one of the old Scots roses, smelling as delicious, but flowering all season in softest pink.

Ideas for its use This would make a lovely surround for a small parterre like the one on page 117, or for a pool like the one on page 108, but would also be lovely as borders to a garden path, with a rose arch or two for some height.

1 *Chrysanthemum parthenium* (feverfew)
2 *Nepeta* 'Six Hills' (catmint)
3 *Dianthus* 'Rainbow Loveliness' (pink)
4 *Rosa* 'Ballerina'
5 *Rosa* 'Felicia'
6 *Digitalis* 'Excelsior' (foxglove)
7 *Pyrus salicifolia* (silver-leaved pear)

Planting 17 Smart leaves for damp and shade

If you can get the foliage in a garden right first, then you're sure of delight, and the rest can look after itself. Here's an example in Glentarg in late June: linear grassy leaves contrasting wonderfully with the broad hostas and palmate rodgersias, set off with a touch of variegation in the honesty, and the interesting tiered foliage of the lily. The combination makes a glamorous planting in which the flower colours are also neatly harmonised, in shades of purple.

Developments and the seasons   There is plenty going on here for most of the season, for those who enjoy fairly restrained plantings. The honesties start flowering in early May, and the flowers are followed in summer by silvery seed pods. The rodgersia foliage turns striking shades of scarlet and rust brown in October; their flower plumes are showy in August, too. The honesty pods and the allium heads both dry well for winter arrangements indoors.

Site   This planting would do best in damp shade, though all the plants here will tolerate anywhere but fullest sun and bone-dry soil.

Maintenance and cost   This lovely and inexpensive scheme couldn't be much simpler without losing the look. The honesties will look fun until autumn, but as the honesty is a biennial, leave plenty of seedlings (do not worry if they are not variegated towards the end of the first season), or grow some on in the vegetable patch and move them into the border for their second year.

Props and additions   This planting would look beautiful beside open water: a pool, a water butt or a water tank. In a sunny enough spot, pots of pink-flowered 'Mrs Quilter' geraniums would harmonise well, as would something grand with scented leaves like the tender balsam *Cedronella triphylla*, with its dusky pinkish flowers, or the hardy anise hyssop.

Substitutions   You could have an even grander rodgersia like *Rodgersia pinnata* 'Elegans'. Other

hostas that might work as well include the many varieties of *Hosta fortunei*. You could also use the beautiful white martagon lily (but not the scarlet varieties). Pale yellow lilies would also look good, especially with some of the greeny-yellow hostas and ferns (try *Osmunda regalis*).

Ideas for its use   This would suit the shadiest part of a garden, or a shaded patio, particularly if it were around a pool or pond, or in a boggy part of the garden by a ditch (if you are lucky enough to have one).

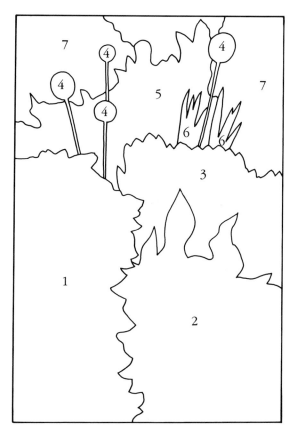

1 *Rodgersia aesculifolia*
2 *Hosta* 'Thomas Hogg'
3 *Iris sibirica* (Siberian iris)
4 *Allium giganteum* (onion)
5 *Lunaria annua* 'Variegata' (honesty)
6 *Iris pseudacorus* (yellow flag iris)
7 *Lilium martagon* (Turk's-cap lily)

Planting 18 Relaxed informality with old roses
in light shade

This planting, part of the garden around a lovely and ancient turreted house in Aberdeen, is put together with a painter's eye. The whole garden, photographed in early July, is a delight, filled with interesting plants, often rescued from oblivion, and still (even after many years) in the course of development and change. I liked this section especially for its freshness of approach, lovely 'feel' and (apart from the double field geranium) simplicity of planting. The ancient rose, *Rosa gallica*, though prone to mildew, is among the most strongly perfumed of them all.

Developments and the seasons Broad sweeps of rich yellow aconites could start the season,

followed by daffodils (perhaps something simple like the lent lily, *Narcissus pseudonarcissus*, or a grand old double like 'Van Sion'), and then as many pheasant's-eye narcissi as possible. Keep most of the yellow away from the young malus leaves; amber or rusty red tulips would be good there. Not visible in the photograph is the blazing scarlet *Lychnis chalcedonica* planted among the campanulas. This is an excellent use of this difficult plant: the dashes of red look wonderful among the silvery blue.

Site This planting is quite shaded by overhanging trees, and would thrive at the margins of light woodland, shrubbery or orchard.

1 *Iris sibirica* (Siberian iris)
2 *Rosa gallica* 'Rosa Mundi'
3 *Filipendula rubra*
4 *Lysimachia punctata*
5 *Campanula lactiflora* (bellflower)
6 *Geranium pratense* 'Flore-pleno' (meadow crane's bill)
7 *Malus* 'Royalty'

ON PLAN ONLY
A *Rosa* 'Maiden's Blush'
B *Rosa* 'Boule de Neige'
C *Hemerocallis lilio-asphodelus*
D *Vinca minor* 'Caerulea-plena'
E *Athyrium filix-femina*
F *Waldsteinia ternata*

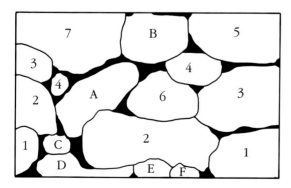

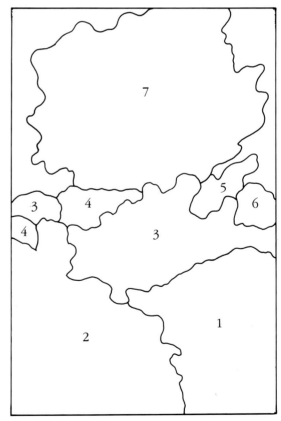

Maintenance and cost The roses, deeply planted in this garden, and on their own roots, spread rather and need to be thinned out now and again. In places, they have also reverted to the original *R. gallica*, though these are lovely too, and just as strongly scented. You might want to prune them out.

Props and additions Any suitably rural seating would do: unvarnished teak or even oak would be especially good. Here, the seating is mostly heavily faded deckchairs.

Substitutions This relaxed and informal planting has some unusual colour associations. The rose, marvellously striped and heavily scented, works perfectly in this setting, and seems not to get mildew so far north. If you wanted something with a longer season, you could just get away with some of the rugosas, perhaps 'Roserie de l'Hay' or 'Sarah Van Fleet'. A soft pink day lily like 'Pink Damask' would be good too. You might prefer *Lysimachia ciliata*, instead of the strong yellow of *L. punctata*, but it is harder to find.

Ideas for its use With a few other roses as shown on the ground plan (or 'Chapeau de Napoleon' and 'Fantin Latour'), the depth of the bed could be increased, and the campanula planted at the back of the filipendula. A fence or trellis behind it could be covered with roses like 'Alister Stella Gray' and 'Zéphïrine Drouhin', or, if there is room, the malus or a silver-leaved willow like *Salix alba* 'Argentea', or even the glaucous blue *S.* 'Nancy Saunders'.

Container Gardens

A plant growing in a pot always looks different from the same thing growing in the open ground. Container-grown plants are on display, and can usually be moved around the garden until you find exactly the spot where they will make most impact. The larger the container the less mobile it is, but large pots are also worth having, not only because they look grand but because they can accommodate a variety of plants. This makes them almost like flower arrangements, or even miniature gardens in their own right.

The original idea of using pots was to let gardeners grow tender plants which needed to be brought indoors, or at least into the orangery, over winter. They still look best when holding plants that are unsuitable for the open garden, whether these are traditional things like lemons, myrtles and oleanders (and rosemary and lavender in the colder parts of Europe and North America) or newer things like cannas, verbenas and rare salvias.

The containers shown here vary from old copper boilers to grand Italian pots, but all the plants will grow just as happily in a half-oildrum or an old paint can. The paint can might almost be better than Tuscan terracotta in some ways, for if you forget to empty it of plants in time, or bring it indoors for the winter, at least it will not crack when the soil in it freezes. Earthenware pots too big to carry indoors or be stored out of the cold need to be emptied each autumn (most of the half-hardy flora shown here root easily from cuttings, so overwinter plenty of cuttings rather than the summer's vast plants). They can then be turned upside down so

that water runs off them easily. Any really valuable pots should of course be stored indoors.

If you have too little space to allow indoor storage, use wooden tubs or some of the better fibreglass ones, which can stand some expansion from freezing soil. Another alternative, if you want grand containers, is to find those with zinc or plastic liners to hold the soil and the plants. Some well-organised gardeners have various sets of plantings in spare liners, so that when they are bored with one set, or the plantings go over, they can simply slot a new set of plants into place.

Most of the plantings shown here are of mixtures, but there are many other ways of displaying plants in containers. For example, sometimes having one thing by itself in abundance will provide some contrast with the more complicated plantings. Try, for instance, *Argyranthemum* 'Vancouver', a lovely pink Paris daisy that will grow exuberantly in almost any size of container. It is also worth having a few moveable pots of easy annuals and fragrant flowers like night-scented stock, mignonette (keep both well fed), or even some of the scented-leaf geraniums, to have by the steps, or the study door, or wherever you spend time.

Tall plants such as standard bays, lemon trees, some of the bigger lilies and roses, should always be planted in proper soil (such as John Innes compost No. 4). This is much heavier than peat-based compost, and helps keep the container on the ground in a high wind. (Pots break with great ease if blown over.) Anything fast-growing and floppy, like the helichrysums, argyranthemums and verbenas, will thrive in lightweight composts, and will keep growing if fed regularly (at least weekly) after the first two months or so, when the compost's nutrients will be running out. Though all these can be used in elegant 'arrangements', they can also look wonderful by themselves in as big a pot as you can manage. The best of the verbenas for growing by itself (the other named sorts don't work well in anything much larger than 30 cm (1 ft) or so in diameter), is the bushy one usually called 'Sissinghurst'.

In winter, once the half-hardies are finished, you could fill your containers with hardy evergreen plants from elsewhere in the garden. Ivies are good; something like 'Green Ripple' or the prettily variegated 'Silver Queen'. You could add a topiary box plant, or even something that the Victorians loved – a young monkey puzzle tree.

Since the discovery of the vast and delectable flora broadly classed as 'alpines', containers have been used for those too. Many gardeners hunger for stone troughs in which to grow them, though such plantings would often look better with a model railway bridge or two added. It is easier, just as decorative and very much cheaper, simply to keep a few flat earthenware pans of sempervivums (especially the gorgeous purple-leaved 'Lady Kelly') for decorating steps, and small and delightful things like *Origanum rotundifolium* 'Kent Beauty', with its frilly amethyst cones of bracts.

Another alternative use for tubs is to grow things you must have in your garden, but for which you cannot provide the right soil. If you love hydrangeas, or azaleas (and some of the scented ones related to the marvellous yellow *Rhododendron luteum* are lovely), and you live on whitest chalk, grow them in tubs of peaty soil.

The chief maintenance problem for all tubs, pots and containers is watering (except for things like geraniums which will not mind drying out). Even pots 1 m (1 yd) across, with a big planting, will need two or three gallons of water a day in hot weather.

Planting 19 Two contrasting plants for a small pot

This charming mixture for a small pot or two is shown here in July at Crossing House, where Margaret Fuller's wonderful and tight-packed garden, expanding along the railway tracks between Shepreth and Cambridge, is open to the public (see also page 47). Mrs Fuller claimed that the little perennial toadflax had seeded itself, and the resulting combination of delicate green and rich red fleshy leaves, highlighted by the pale pink toadflax flowers, is pleasing indeed. This garden is worth a visit at any time of year.

Developments and the seasons   The houseleek flowers in July; the toadflax keeps going for the entire season.

Site   This planting would succeed in either sun or dappled shade.

Maintenance and cost   The toadflax seeds itself once it is well established. It is also suitable for pavements, steps and crannies in walls. The sempervivum flower stalk can be removed after flowering, leaving the succulent rosettes.

Substitutions   Almost any of the grander sempervivums would do; this reddish one is attractive, but it is the contrast between the architecture of its leaves and the delicacy of the toadflax that is so pretty. Another good sempervivum here would be the purple 'Lady Kelly'.

Ideas for its use   A decorative concrete container has been used here, but the plants would also look good in a flat earthenware pan, by steps, a doorway or pool, or even grown together in crannies on a wallhead.

Sempervivum hybrid red-leaved (houseleek)
Cymbalaria muralis 'Alba' (ivy-leaved toadflax)

Planting 20 Building big effects with tiny units

A luxuriant effect is not always achieved by using big pots: this lovely arrangement of many different pelargonium varieties, in an imaginatively planted and rather grand garden at Jenkyn Place in Hampshire, simply uses an extravagant number of small pots. It is also good gardening practice, since pelargoniums (commonly known as geraniums) run to leaf with too much root room. It is not only a feast for the eye, but also for the nose: some of the scented-leaf pelargoniums are delicious. If you visit, ask for directions to John Coke's nearby 'Green Farm Plants', one of the most interesting nurseries in the country.

Developments and the seasons This will look marvellous throughout the growing season. Geraniums are tough plants: if you do not have a greenhouse or enough windowsill space to overwinter them, they can be dried off, wrapped in newspaper, and stored packed in boxes, somewhere cold but frost-free.

Site This planting needs some direct sunshine. It also needs to be sheltered: any wind will wreak havoc. Geraniums grow well in flat pans, too, and these are more wind tolerant.

Maintenance and cost Use soil rather than peat-based composts: the plants will need the extra weight down below to keep them upright. Here, the 'wall' of soft colours is created by the ascending stone steps of the sundial. For a similar effect, stand the pots on bricks arranged in tiers, or use large pots towards the centre. Geraniums flower best in poor soil, so do not overfeed them. Some of these plants are several years old, so a good number of

them should be overwintered whole, not just as pots of cuttings.

Props and additions Several firms (see Sarah Cotton's guide to specialist nurseries listed in the bibliography) make perfectly acceptable sundials if you do not have an antique one to hand. Scrub new ones with mud slurry (mixed with soot if you have it), then brush it off when dry, to create an instant aged effect. Earthenware pots of this scale are once again becoming more popular than the ubiquitous bright brown plastic. Your local potter might also be making some interesting things.

Substitutions This handsome grouping is very flexible; its richness is given as much by the variation of the leaves as by the flowers. Though tempting, avoid using too many 'regal' pelargoniums, since they flower only in one short, if magnificent, burst. The only regal you should not do without is the sumptuous plummy black 'Lord Bute'.

Ideas for its use Ignore the grand gates and steps: this planting could work perfectly in a small and rather formal enclosure such as a patio or paved front garden.

Pelargoniums, including:
Ivy-leaved: 'La France', 'L'Elegante', 'White Mesh'
Zonals (these have exotic leaf colours): 'Mrs Quilter', 'Golden Harry Hieover' (both in gold and red), 'Crystal Palace Gem' (gold and light green), 'Caroline Schmidt', 'Mrs Parker' (white, greens and some bronze)
Regals (these have a single burst of flowers): especially 'Lord Bute' (blackish burgundy flowers), 'Joan Morf'
Scented-leaf geraniums: especially 'Rose of Bengal', 'Prince of Orange', 'Queen of Lemons', 'Sweet Mimosa' and 'Lady Plymouth'

Planting 21 Simple grandeur for a large container

The planting of this tub, one of a row of several at Hidcote, near Chipping Campden in Gloucestershire, works wonderfully with its surroundings – the dusky red of the geraniums, the silvery yellow of the helichrysum, and the soft blue of the boarding behind it – and demonstrates that successful colour schemes do not begin and end with plants but must take account of other nearby elements.

Developments and the seasons Amongst the exuberant growth are a few red-brown leaves of the foliage plant called iresine, which give a touch of late spring colour. If you prefer colour from flowers, some good scarlet tulips would provide early cheer, but do not put the tub out too soon or a snap frost might ruin the planting altogether. This abundance is more than a season old, and shows that it is worth trying to overwinter the whole thing.

Site This planting needs plenty of sun for a good part of the day.

Maintenance and cost Initial costs of the plants are quite low, but tubs like this might be expensive. These tubs – almost certainly old lemon tubs – are very grand, having not only loops for moving them (poles placed through the loops enable two or four people to carry them indoors at the end of the season) but also hinged sides, so that the soil can be renewed without having to move the plants themselves.

Props and additions This would look just as good in half a barrel, and possibly grander still in 'Versailles' tubs or something similar. White ones would need to be painted slatey blue or greyish green.

Substitutions Against these blue-painted walls, the red of the pelargonium is especially effective. Scarlet would be vulgar, pink a bit too sweet; another rather dusky red one is 'Du Barry'. There are some good white 'zonals' too, like the semi-double 'Hermione' – though the purple iresine foliage plant would need to be more prominent. You could use the attractive and subtle variegated form of this helichrysum.

Ideas for its use The container needs to be quite large – at least 55 cm (18 in) square – to achieve this luxuriant look. That rather limits where you place it. Here, several of them are placed against a grand barn wall. Four in a modest yard would have the same effect.

1 *Pelargonium* 'Burton's Variety'
2 *Helichrysum petiolatum* 'Limelight' or 'Sulphureum'
3 *Iresine lindenii*

Planting 22 Topiary fun

This golden cockerel shows that small-scale topiary can be fun and decorative, and does not have to be 'washing mops' of box, or tiny bay obelisks. Its owners, both artists, garden with great panache round a Georgian building that is more pavilion than house, with wonderful views over the River Tweed at Kelso, in the Scottish borders. Other pictures are on page 130.

Developments and the seasons Topiary is seasonless, and so if you have a small garden and want the planting to change more through the year, you could add to the underplanting in the pot.

Site This charming creature, four years old, stands in dappled shade, but would do just as well in more sun. It would then, of course, need watering more often.

Maintenance and cost The bird is clipped when necessary. Four stout struts of wire gave the young plant its basic shape, the owners' imagination and the plant's vigour supplying the later flesh. It would be possible, if you wanted a simpler planting beneath the bird, to opt for dense ground cover, perhaps Corsican mint (*Mentha requienii*), which gives a brilliant and wonderfully perfumed mat of emerald green, or either the green or gold form of

Lysimachia nummularia (creeping Jenny), unless you find the flowers too egg-yolk yellow. There's also a charming and truly named pinkish daisy, called *Bellium minutum*, that would look pretty. This potted bird is not something that you can forget to water, as so much love and effort goes into it.

Props and additions This is in an old copper container, but the bird would look quite as well nested in a square tub, even a white one. Earthenware containers look better with flowers than with topiary.

Substitutions This golden bird could also have been made using the plain green lonicera, or one of the gold or silver variegated boxes, which would give a slightly denser look, but take twice as long to build. Other topiary animals in this garden are of plain green box.

Ideas for its use In less exuberant gardens this might be better against a plainer background: a hedge (even of green *Lonicera nitida*) or a sheet of a good ivy. It would make a striking centrepiece for a square of lawn, or a focal point in the angle of a pathway or by a doorway (perhaps as one of an unmatched pair), if the planting nearby was not too complex.

1 *Lonicera nitida* 'Baggesen's Gold' (evergreen honeysuckle)
2 *Cineraria maritima*
3 *Anthemis cupaniana*
4 *Paeonia lactiflora* 'Sarah Bernhardt' (herbaceous paeony)
5 *Nepeta* 'Six Hills' (catmint)

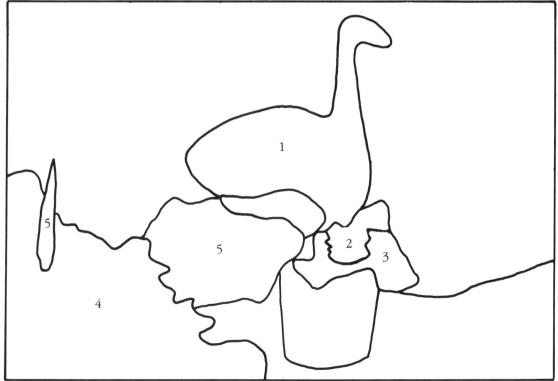

Herbaceous Borders

I have a passion for herbaceous flowers (the ones that die back to the ground each autumn and, sensibly, overwinter more or less underground) whether they are combined into grand or modest borders, or are mixed with roses and shrubs. After being vilified for years, when everyone thought that ericas, dwarf conifers and ground-cover plants were the only sort of gardening, everyone seems again to want delphiniums, hollyhocks, lilies and asters. Certainly, the herbaceous flora is a mine of wonders, providing a wide range of colour (as subtle or as loud as you like), over most of the growing season, and especially at the time when you will most want to be outside in the garden.

Colourful flowers are of course the main *raison d'être* of herbaceous gardening, with much less interest in the decorative value of the leaves. However, colour almost always needs some sort of strategy behind its use, and it is not enough to cram a mixture of brightly coloured things together and hope that it works. Most gardeners avoid the problems by choosing pale flowers (and there are some lovely pale borders in the following pages), but brightly coloured schemes can work if you go for the *fauve*, and use the brightest things you can find. Hang them together as colour harmonies rather than clashes (there are some good examples of these, too). If you find this alarming, it is always possible to use greys, silvers, and so on to unify a shaky scheme, though you might find that some gardeners sniff if they see too much *Artemisia* 'Powys Castle' or 'Valerie Finnis'.

If you have a bit of spare garden, you could try a border devoted to one sort of plant. The border shown on page 87 is mostly delphiniums, which took my breath away with its colourfulness. Another colourful border could be made just of lupins, which smell wonderful when in flower. Shades of pink, with a few blue plants, look particularly good, backed by a nice beech hedge. In smaller gardens, where it is not practical to use such short-season flowers, sow a quick-growing annual (say *Phacelia tanacetifolia*, or scented and soft blue *Asperula azurea*), to cover the bare earth after the lupins are cut back in late June or July. Alternatively, you could interleave the lupins with a mass of yellow and lemon kniphofias – another group of plants returning to favour, and flowering later in the summer.

Even in a tiny garden, a herbaceous planting is possible. It would be wonderful to wrap a lush herbaceous border (it needs to be at least 2 m (6 ft) deep, if possible, and preferably twice that for real luxuriance) around a small lawn or piece of brick paving. Long, narrow town gardens could consist only of two long herbaceous borders and a central path with a nice seat at the end, or a rustic pavilion if you're handy with a saw and nails (a friend, whose garden is shown on page 90, made a charming one out of a few posts and bark offcuts from the sawmill; it only cost a few pounds, and is a lot more fun than fancy ones in fibreglass).

New gardeners also worry about the work involved in growing herbaceous plants. While the immense borders of the great Edwardian gardens did take up vast amounts of gardeners' labour, you can still get good effects without a staff of twenty. Though the garden on page 87 does have a few gardeners to help (delphiniums, even the sturdiest, must always be staked), the one on page 78 is maintained entirely by its owners. While a well-planned border will be in flower continuously from June until the end of the season, the individual plants that it contains have a short season, and there will always be something that has just finished flowering and is looking awful. Borders do need regular tidying and a certain amount of weeding and feeding if at all possible, but the rewards, when you see your border by the dappled golden light of a summer evening (when, in any case, you can't see the bits you've forgotten to tidy), are immense.

Planting 23 Colourful extravagance at Powys Castle

Powys Castle in Wales (photographed in mid-July) has perhaps one of the most enviable of all garden sites in this book: an astonishing sequence of seventeenth-century terraces, steps and grottos, now stripped of their parterres and reworked as grand herbaceous borders, extravagantly planted and almost over-rich in species. The view out over the vale is spectacular too, and it becomes hard to know where to look next. Many National Trust gardens are rather dull; this is not one of them. Amongst many lovely pieces of planting, I thought this section would make a splendid and long-lasting display in a small garden; much more fun than a tiny lawn or square of gravel.

Developments and the seasons You could easily add a bulb planting to this scheme, watching out for the bulbs when the border is pulled to pieces every couple of seasons (otherwise the clumps of herbaceous plants grow too large and starve). The scheme as shown here in mid-July will flower until September, and the fuchsia will keep going until heavy frosts. The flask-shaped rose hips are a glossy glowing red in autumn.

Site This planting is on a sunny terrace, though the light shading of the trees behind it gives the hint it would do well in moderate shade.

Maintenance and cost This planting needs lifting every couple of years, for thinning and replanting. It will need weeding now and again, though the denser the planting the less this will be necessary. The low box hedge at the front of the border needs regular trimming. The alstroemerias can be bought, though they are easy from seed – one seed per small pot, sown while there are still frosts, or put in the fridge. The flower stems of the wonderful *Crambe cordifolia* need to be cut out once the vast sprays of tiny honey-scented flowers are finished; they go brown and are very untidy.

Props and additions As the overall tones are pale, and there is plenty of greenery, white seats (if sufficiently skeletal in design) would look fine, seats painted slate blue even more so. The planting would suit a trellis arbour, draped with honeysuckles and white roses to bring more perfume into the garden, but do not have much more in the way of fancy props; tubs of topiary are about all.

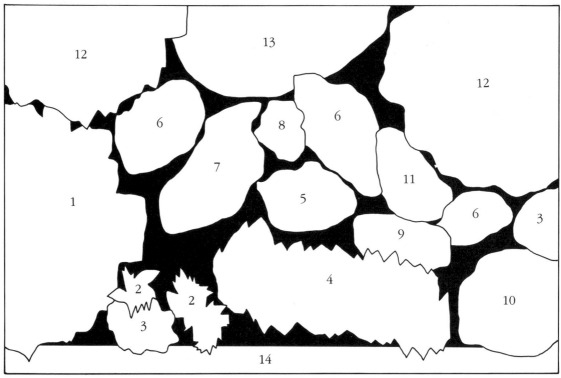

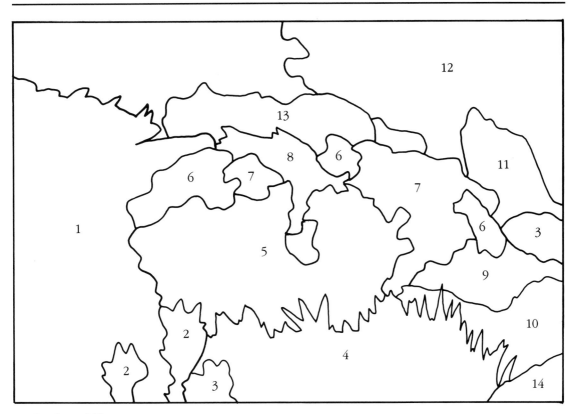

1 *Crambe cordifolia*
2 *Lilium* 'Destiny' (lily)
3 *Penstemon* 'Garnet'
4 *Crocosmia* 'Lady Hamilton'
5 *Hemerocallis* 'Dorothy McDade'
6 *Monarda* 'Croftway Scarlet' (sweet bergamot)
7 *Alstroemeria Ligtu* hybrids (Peruvian lily)
8 *Kniphofia* 'Atlanta'
9 *Anthemis sancta-Johanis*
10 *Achillea taygetea* 'Moonshine' (yarrow)
11 *Cichorium intybus*
12 *Rosa* 'Moyesii' (species rose)
13 *Fuchsia magellanica*
14 *Buxus sempervirens* (common box)

Substitutions   This colourful planting would succeed with many substitutions. For example, any day lily could be used, from ochre yellow through to some of the dusky pinks (which might even be better). Some good clumps of white lilies (preferably scented, like *Lilium candidum* or *L. longiflorum*), could be planted instead of the yellow one, and the kniphofia could be the majestic *Kniphofia* 'Lord Roberts' in rosy orange.

Ideas for its use   In a small garden (especially an urban one), this would look splendid against an ivy-covered wall or fence, where the pale colours would sing in front of the darkness. It would also look good attached to a planting of hostas like the one on page 12.

Planting 24 Cottage-garden lushness with simple flowers

This simple yet lush planting, shown here in June, forms part of a much-loved kitchen garden attached to a farmhouse at Edzell. Lavish attention (and manure) ensure that the simplest of plants, put together with care, make a stunning show. The garden is overlooked by the road leading to the ruins of Edzell Castle with its own astonishing walled 'pleasance', so that the public can share in its pleasures. The border is probably as much as 5 m (15 ft) deep, one of the deepest included in this book. This gives it great richness. The colour scheme is mainly of blues, mauves and pinks, with touches of scarlet and yellow.

Developments and the seasons Nothing much happens in this border until the middle of June or so, and then it is constantly in flower until the end of September. In a small garden, flowers for early spring should be kept near the house, perhaps in pots.

Site This planting is south facing and in full sun, though all the plants would tolerate light shade. Rich soil is required: the soil here is generously fed from the byres, but you could use chemical fertilisers and peat or similar nutrients and soil conditioners.

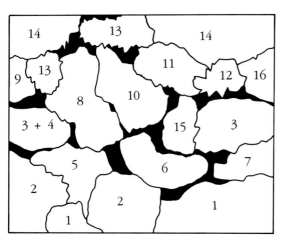

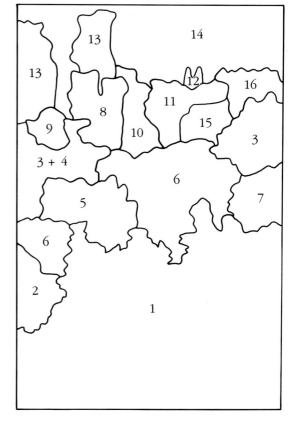

1 *Centaurea dealbata*
2 *Kentranthus ruber* (valerian)
3 *Pyrethrum roseum* pink form
4 *Pyrethrum roseum* red form
5 *Solidagos* (golden rod)
6 *Aster* (species)
7 *Lysimachia punctata*
8 *Papaver orientale* pink seedling (Oriental poppy)
9 *Polemonium foliosissimum* (Jacob's ladder)
10 *Papaver orientale* scarlet form (Oriental poppy)
11 *Aquilegia* long-spurred hybrids
12 *Lupinus* white (lupin)
13 *Delphinium* hybrid seedlings
14 *Rosa* 'Nevada' (modern shrub rose)
15 *Lychnis chalcedonica* (Cross of Jerusalem)
16 *Achillea* variety (yarrow)

Maintenance and cost Borders on this scale are hard work, and this one must have almost daily attention. The rewards are, of course, correspondingly high. One of the charms of this planting is that hardly any of the flowers are rare or grand. Ordinary things, well looked after, generously planted, and cleverly put together can make marvellous gardens.

Props and additions Low box hedges border the beds in this garden, which contains a few sheds and, among strawberries, large earthenware farm drains up-ended to make flowerpots. If you want to have seats on the grass so you can look at all this glorious planting, they should probably be in natural timber, and suitably rustic. White furniture is too brash and would spoil the scene.

Substitutions The colour scheme of this farmhouse border could be kept going for the whole season. So many plants here are easy to grow from seed that there is almost no need for substitutes. *Lysimachia ciliata* 'runs' less vigorously than *L. punctata*, and is a softer yellow. There are many named sorts of Oriental poppy to be found; white poppies would also look good here. Elsewhere in the border, beyond the picture's limits, pink lupins and masses of blue campanulas add to the effect.

Ideas for its use This lovely cottage-garden planting would look fine in the front garden of the right sort of house. With apple trees along a broad grass path, it could also make a charming backyard planting, perhaps with vegetables beyond the screen of roses.

Planting 25 Small-scale magic for a warm corner

I found this enchanting small-scale planting outside the courtyard of Broughton Castle, made with a mixture of the ancient and the very modern. It has a fresh and magical look, like a piece of sophisticated medieval tapestry, and shows that herbaceous planting need not be lush and costly.

Developments and the seasons This is a good long-season planting, but is at its best in July and August when the yellow foxglove and the phlox are in flower. The half-hardies – the cosmos, salvias and bidens – and the violas will keep flowering until the first frost. For flowers in April and May you could plant pasque flowers (*Pulsatilla vulgaris* in either the original purple, or a grand white or even grander burgundy) and anemones, as well as small species tulips. The white, flushed red flowers of the lady tulip (*Tulipa clusiana*) would be especially good here.

Site This planting is at the base of a sunny wall (wreathed in soft pink roses), and needs plenty of warmth and moisture. Everything would also succeed in moderate shade.

Maintenance and cost Such dense planting makes maintenance fairly straightforward. The Blessed thistle is biennial, which means that it flowers (untidily) in its second season. The best foliage is on young plants, so it needs to be replaced each year. It is possible to save their seeds if your garden, and the summer, is warm – though it's simpler to buy anew. The digitalis is reasonably perennial. The wonderful cosmos used to be expensive, though it's now being produced by tissue culture, and can be expected to become much easier to find. In mild gardens it will survive outdoors all winter. In cold gardens, the *Cosmos atrosanguinea* (with flowers such a dark burgundy as to be almost black, and smelling wonderfully of chocolate), and the *Bidens ferulaefolia* (which also makes a lovely plant for pots or window boxes), need to be lifted (or have divisions or cuttings taken), and overwintered. The silybum (which next year will produce tall heads of exceptionally spiny thistles), digitalis and violas are all easy to grow from seed.

Props and additions In this garden, ornate Victorian cast-iron seats and antique marble benches decorate the scene. But this planting is deceptively unsophisticated, so anything would do, even the simple and rusty. A few pots of lilies would be pleasant additions on either side, and so would a hosta or two.

Substitutions You could use the yellow *Digitalis lutea* instead of the one here, though its flowers are smaller. The white phlox is lovely, though almost any of the varieties would look pretty. Nothing could replace the thistle, the cosmos or the pretty bidens.

Ideas for its use This would look lovely in an orchard garden, particularly under cherries: the bronze violas would match red fruits prettily, and the planting would continue to look well under the hazy bronze of the autumn cherry foliage. This bed could also be wrapped around a circular cobbled area, centred on a big pot like the one on page 71.

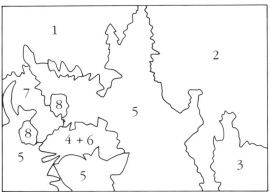

1 *Phlox* 'White Admiral'
2 *Silybum marianum* (Blessed thistle)
3 *Cosmos atrosanguineus*
4 *Viola* 'Arkwright Ruby'
5 *Digitalis ambigua* (yellow foxglove)
6 *Bidens ferulaefolia*
7 *Salvia nemorosa* 'Superba'
8 *Viola cornuta* blue and white forms

PLAN: No plan given; simply use three plants of each species.

Planting 26 Dense planting in cool colours

Playing safe with plenty of white flowers combined with soft blues and pinks, we crammed plants into this border for a quick effect: here it is in its second season. Such dense planting will look luxuriant very quickly, but after the third season will need a great deal of thinning out. Part of the interest of herbaceous borders at their best is that they seem to hover at the boundary of chaos. They are constantly changing and, if you keep on top of them, provide constant delight too. This border has been made in an old walled garden which has ancient espaliered apples that have fallen away from the walls.

Developments and the seasons Early in the season, the beds are filled with *Narcissus triandrus* and the tulip 'White Triumphator', followed by camassias. After the burst of June flowering shown here, penstemons ('Apple Blossom', 'Hidcote Pink', and 'Sour Grapes') keep the colour scheme going, aided by lavenders and the wonderful aromatic-leaved *Caryopteris clandonensis* (the best form is

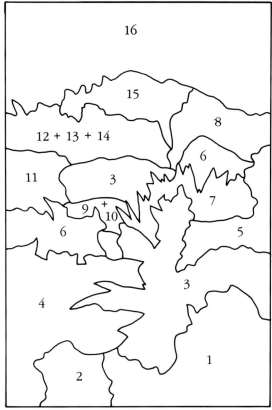

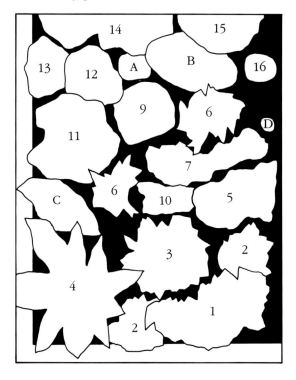

1 *Salvia officinalis* narrow-leaved form (sage)
2 *Viola cornuta* 'Lilacina' (horned viola)
3 *Artemisia* 'Powys Castle'
4 *Acanthus mollis* (bear's breeches)
5 *Geranium pratense* 'Flore-pleno' white form
6 *Rosa* 'Tuscany Superb' (old rose, gallica)
7 *Iris* 'Aline'
8 *Campanula latiloba* 'Alba' (bellflower)
9 *Geranium macrorrhizum* 'Album' (crane's-bill)
10 *Aquilegia* double pink form (columbine)
11 *Ballota* Cretan form
12 *Campanula persicifolia* white (peach-leaved campanula)
13 *Penstemon* 'Glabra'
14 *Nepeta* 'Six Hills Giant' (catmint)
15 *Lupinus* 'Rose Queen' (lupin)
16 Apple tree

ON PLAN ONLY
A *Phlox* 'Nora Leigh'
B *Matthiola* 'White perennial' (stock)
C *Sphaeralcea munroana*
D *Rosa* 'Mme Isaac Pereire'

'Kew Blue', unless you like very hazy colours). Against the wall, the deep pink rose 'Mme Isaac Pereire' has a second wave of flowers in September.

Site This planting is in a west-facing border and light sandy soil. It would tolerate a little more shade, although you might begin to lose the sages and artemisias (in which case, use more penstemons and the aromatic, daisy-like *Anthemis cupaniana*).

Maintenance and cost If necessary in a smaller garden, leave out some of the campanulas. Don't leave out the stock; it smells too good for that. Remember to save some seed, just in case you have no self-sown seedlings. The dense planting, while giving a fast effect, means that some of the smaller things are quickly shaded out unless you thin or cut back the larger plants.

Props and additions You could add pots of agapanthus, the wonderful mahogany-red forms

of shrubby *Mimulus* (sometimes listed as *Diplacus*), *cupreus* and *Verbena* 'Hidcote Purple', or the deep china-blue flowers of *Convolvulus mauretanica*. The seats nearby are painted a greenish blue, though slate-blue or grey would be better.

Substitutions The irises are pale blue and scented; white or even ochre yellow (say, 'Lord Warden') would be as nice, or the ancient *Iris florentina* in iced white, and with a heady perfume. The narrow-leaved sage is a particularly floriferous form that can also be used in the kitchen; other forms could be used instead. If the double white geranium is hard to find, use a single white, or *Geranium sylvaticum* 'Album'.

Ideas for its use Not shown in the picture is the low box hedge dividing the bed from the grass; this could also be used to wrap it round a small lawn or brick patio; and the architectural framework will also tighten up the bareness of the design over winter. This border could be combined with a hot planting like the one on page 75.

Planting 27 Simplicity and plenty for full sun

This is another section of the splendid and well-kept border at Edzell Mains, and is good enough in its own right to make a separate planting. Again, it is a pretty mixture of simple flowers, seen here in July, with the blues of the catmints and campanulas spiked with, but not thrown off balance by, scarlet, bronze and yellow.

Developments and the seasons For more late colour, you could add autumn-flowering kniphofias, especially the wonderful pale lemon-yellow 'Percy's Pride', though there are plenty of other good ones, and penstemons like 'Hidcote Pink' and 'Glabra'. You could also usefully add some asters.

1 *Nepeta* 'Six Hills Giant' (catmint)
2 *Campanula persicifolia* 'Telham Beauty' (peach-leaved campanula)
3 *Lysimachia punctata*
4 *Helenium* 'Moerheim Beauty'
5 *Geranium pratense* 'Flore-pleno' (double meadow crane's-bill)
6 *Helianthus* variety (sunflower)
7 *Rudbeckia hirta* (black-eyed Susan)
8 *Lychnis chalcedonica* (Cross of Jerusalem)
9 *Sidalcea* 'Sussex Beauty'
10 *Chrysanthemum maximum* (Shasta daisy).
11 *Achillea filipendulina* (yarrow)
12 *Delphinium* seedling
13 *Rosa* 'Nevada'
14 *Rosa* 'Virginia'
15 *Rosa* 'Pauls Lemon Pillar'
16 *Kentranthus ruber* (valerian)

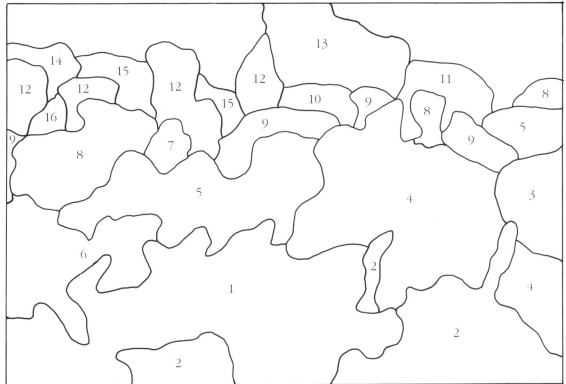

Site This planting receives full sun and is fed regularly. Being in Aberdeenshire, it will last longer than it would in the far south.

Maintenance and cost The planting needs a certain grand untidiness to look its best, and so maintenance consists mainly of feeding and weeding. There is not much staking to do, though the delphiniums need some help, and the scarlet lychnis may need staking if you can get it to grow as tall as it is here

Props and additions Wooden seats, even park benches, with a few bleached cushions for comfort, would look good, and not too self-conscious.

Substitutions In this painterly planting there is not much need to substitute because things are hard to find. Only the double geranium might not be available. If you would like a few posher things, there are some good double forms of the campanula, especially the marvellously elegant cup-and-saucer forms in both pure white and clear blue; and there is also a double form of the scarlet lychnis, if you can find it, as well as pink or white singles.

Ideas for its use Just out of view is the box hedge that encloses this wonderful tangle and gives it a clear boundary. Part of the border's look is determined by the generosity of it all, and you need a bit of space to do that. In a small garden, the amount of non-productive space like the lawn could be reduced. This planting would also look wonderful around a pool, with a few pots from page 68.

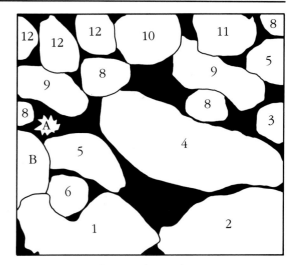

1   *Nepeta* 'Six Hills Giant' (catmint)
2   *Campanula persicifolia* 'Telham Beauty' (peach-leaved campanula)
3   *Lysimachia punctata*
4   *Helenium* 'Moerheim Beauty'
5   *Geranium pratense* 'Flore-pleno' (double meadow crane's-bill)
6   *Helianthus* variety (sunflower)
7   *Rudbeckia hirta* (black-eyed Susan)
8   *Lychnis chalcedonica* (Cross of Jerusalem)
9   *Sidalcea* 'Sussex Beauty'
10 *Chrysanthemum maximum* (Shasta daisy).
11 *Achillea filipendulina* (yarrow)
12 *Delphinium* seedling
13 *Rosa* 'Nevada'
14 *Rosa* 'Virginia'
15 *Rosa* 'Pauls Lemon Pillar'
16 *Kentranthus ruber* (valerian)

ON PLAN ONLY
A   *Kniphofia*
B   *Lupinus* seedling in pink

Planting 28 An old-fashioned border in the grand manner

It's a great surprise to find, in the suburbs of Leeds, a grand border like this; few garden owners think that they could plan on such a scale, or that they could afford to maintain a border like this if they did. What makes this one even more startling is that it is largely devoted to a single sort of plant: the delphinium. This gives the scheme a strong unity, and contributes to its impact. Though this garden does have plenty of gardeners, and the delphinium varieties are either unobtainable or expensive, it would be perfectly possible to grow some lovely things from seed, and to scale the planting down to suit a small garden and a small budget. However, delphiniums do need some hard work, especially in keeping them upright. Though the cost of the bamboo canes might be the largest cost of the garden, this planting is certainly for the brave, though not necessarily for the rich.

Developments and the seasons Unless you want to garden on an even grander scale, it's probably best to keep the usual spring bulbs out of an area like this, and start the season with early flowering herbaceous species such as camassias, *Leucojum aestivum* and *L. vernalis*, pulsatillas and pulmonarias. Add asters like *A. amellus* 'King George' for autumn, when the roses will still be in flower too.

Site This planting needs full sun, good soil and, if at all possible, plenty of shelter.

Maintenance and cost The maintenance here is on a grand scale (and there are other borders adjoining this one). However, a single and spare-time set of hands could easily look after a half to two-thirds of a border like this, providing there wasn't too much else to do. Everything at the back of the borders must be staked. The delphinium 'stools' in this garden are thinned down to eight or nine stalks every spring, and are almost never replaced (conventionally, young shoots are rooted each spring, and used to replace the older plants). The flower spikes are cut a little before the last flowers fade – both for the sake of appearance and to stop seed pods maturing. Slugs are suppressed. Delphiniums grown from seed will become good plants in their second season. Decent phlox cultivars need to be bought.

Props and additions The only props needed would be a rose pergola like the one shown here, and a big seat beneath it.

Substitutions This border is based mainly on two or three genera in which breeding still continues apace, especially among the delphiniums, so this garden changes as the owner looks for good new varieties, while keeping the best of the old. If you find some of the harder blues a bit abrupt against some of the sharp yellows, you could shift the main colour balance to richer, deeper blues, or white, or even amethyst-purples. Some of the detail could be left out – the heuchera, the thymes and, unless you want your garden to look like Monet's marvellous creation at Giverny, the nasturtiums. Instead, you could add more day lilies, and some blue and some straw- and golden-yellow irises.

Ideas for its use Condensed, this would make a charming back garden, with a gravel path as here, or a narrow strip of lawn (with a paved edge so that sprawling plants don't kill the grass). Leave access paths between the delphiniums and the fencing supporting the roses at the back of the border. Even without trees making a background, and with houses instead, it would be a pleasure.

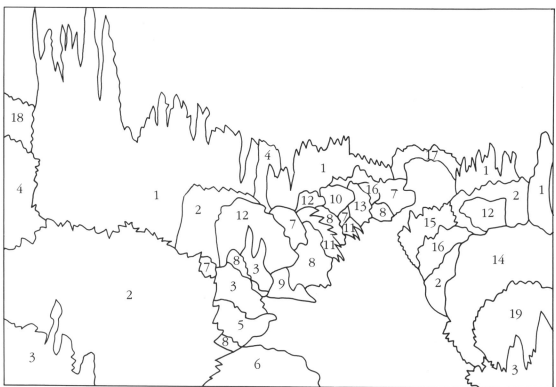

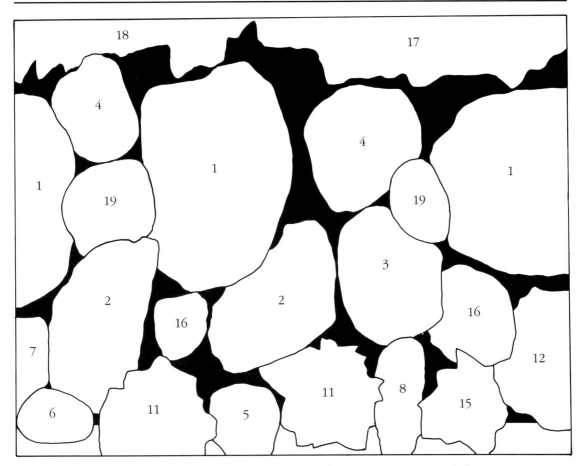

1 *Delphinium* – not all the varieties shown here are commercially available (those that are include: 'Faust', 'Gillian Dallas', 'Sungleam', 'Tiddles', 'Turkish Delight', 'Strawberry Fair')

2 *Phlox* varieties, including 'Border Gem', 'Brigadier', 'Cool of the Evening', 'Dodo Hanbury Forbes', 'Toit de Paris', 'Prince of Orange'

3 *Lupinus* cream (lupin)

4 *Lychnis chalcedonica* (Cross of Jersualem)

5 *Heuchera sanguinea* (coral flower)

6 *Thymus drucei* (thyme)

7 *Achillea ptarmica* 'The Pearl' (sneezewort)

8 *Geranium endressii* (crane's-bill)

9 *Tropaeolum majus* (nasturtium)

10 Sidalceas in variety

11 *Hemerocallis fulva* (day lily)

12 *Anthemis* 'Grallach Gold'

13 *Kentranthus ruber* pink form (Valerian)

14 *Inula occulis-Christi*

15 *Dryopteris filix-mas* (male fern)

16 *Monarda* 'Croftway Pink' (sweet bergamot)

17 *Rosa* 'Albertine'

18 *Rosa* 'Zephyrine Drouhin'

19 *Polemonium foliosissimum*

Planting 29 Green flowers and strong foliage for shade

Although these are mostly herbaceous plants shown here in May, this is not a traditional herbaceous border. David Bromley, in his Shropshire garden, has here mixed a few collectors' plants with old faithfuls, most of them with good foliage, to give an unusually adaptable and long-season planting that would give the smallest space excitement.

Development and the seasons   Not much happens here early on in the season, since it is part of a much larger garden. In small spaces, it would be worth adding some of the fancy celandines (the doubles are great fun) and perhaps some *Anemone blanda* cultivars – 'White Splendour' lives up to its name, though some of the deep blues are wonderful too. This planting starts to flower in late April, and will keep going into early October (the autumn crocuses will give the last burst of flower).

Site   This planting will succeed in quite deep shade – which more ordinary herbaceous flowers would hate. A dampish soil is helpful but not essential.

Maintenance and cost   Many of the plants here are easy to grow from seed, though you will have to buy the euphorbia and the colchicums as plants. The wildly handsome grass (avena), eventually with marvellous tussocks of arching bluish leaves, needs to have its tall flower spikes removed in late summer (unless you want to harvest them earlier, and dry them).

Props and additions   If this planting were built round a small terrace or patio, you could add pots of nice things, perhaps white or pale yellow Ghent azaleas, which are often sweetly fragrant.

Substitutions   Most of the plants here are easy to find and to grow. The colchicum is a large pink-flowered variant of the easy *Colchicum speciosum* and there are plenty of other lovely varieties of this species – the plain white single being especially good. The rather grand euphorbia, whose leaves are deep reddish purple in early spring, could perhaps

1 *Geranium* 'Johnson's Blue' (crane's-bill)
2 *Myosotis alpestris* hybrid (forget-me-not)
3 *Colchicum giganteum* (autumn crocus)
4 *Euphorbia martynii*
5 *Rumex sanguineus* 'Sanguineus' (bloody dock)
6 *Onoclea sensibilis* (sensitive fern)
7 *Iris sibirica* (Siberian iris)
8 *Avena candida*
9 *Meconopsis cambrica* orange form (Welsh poppy)

be switched for the more architectural greenery of *Euphorbia mellifera* (with its lovely sweet scent in late spring), or for the gorgeous scarlet-edged leaves of *E. sikkimensis*. The exotic fern could easily be one of the commoner polypodys.

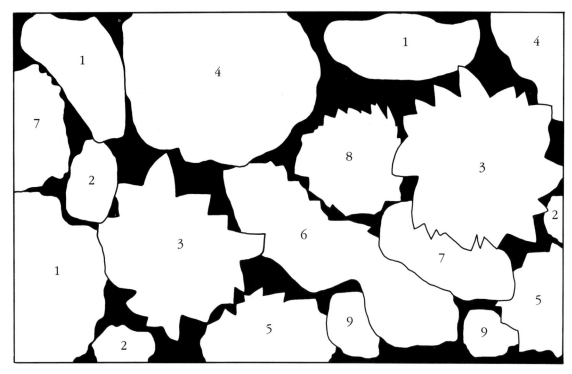

Ideas for its use　The exotic foliage would suit a dark urban garden, and would make a satisfying margin for a paved yard or patio. It could usefully be combined with a pond planting like the one on page 106. It would also be good in the depths of a shrubbery, bordering a path, or under trees (provided that the soil is moist).

1　*Geranium* 'Johnson's Blue' (crane's-bill)
2　*Myosotis alpestris* hybrid (forget-me-not)
3　*Colchicum giganteum* (autumn crocus)
4　*Euphorbia martynii*
5　*Rumex sanguineus* 'Sanguineus' (bloody dock)
6　*Onoclea sensibilis* (sensitive fern)
7　*Iris sibirica* (Siberian iris)
8　*Avena candida*
9　*Meconopsis cambrica* orange form (Welsh poppy)

Planting 30 High summer contrasts for glamorous effects

Here is another luscious and detailed planting from the borders at Powys Castle; in this one, photographed towards the end of July, the contrast between the airy spires of the cimicifuga, the steely barbs of the eryngiums and the rich colours of everything else make for a very heady mixture.

Developments and the seasons With such a dense planting as this, it would be difficult to integrate many spring flowers – though the hellebore will give handsomely gloomy flowers (even in its yellow and pink forms) in early spring. It would be worth using spring-flowering clematis, for example forms of *Clematis alpina* (especially the gorgeous mid-blue 'Columbine') or *C. macropetala*. Earlier remarks on extending the season in herbaceous borders apply here too. Lengthen it late on with a back-screen of suitable roses or honeysuckles (mix *Lonicera sempervirens* with *L. japonica* 'Halliana' for the colour of the first and the smell of the second).

Site Many of the plants shown would be quite happy in shade, though the site here is on a south-facing and sunlit terrace.

Maintenance and cost None of the plants is especially expensive, the clematis being the only ones that might strain the garden budget. The most difficult maintenance problem is how to keep the border looking this luxuriant, without becoming an overcrowded tangle. The clumps, once they've reached optimum size, will thereafter need reducing in size every third season or so. The ground will also need lavish manuring. The plant growth is so lush that weeding won't be a big problem after the first few seasons. Those demanding tasks apart, there is little else to do, except admire your border.

Props and additions Something to give perfume could be planted in pots. Plenty of simple seating is required to allow you to admire your efforts at the planting's peak.

Substitutions The excitement of this border is in the rocketing spikes of the cimicifuga in July and August, so these are essential. It would be possible to use other perennial eryngiums, say *Eryngium planum* or *E. maritimum*, both in shades of steely blue or bluish green, and a pale pink polygonum rather than the hot red one here. Any of the tall aconites, especially pale blue ones like 'Bressingham Spire', would look splendid instead of the faintly grubby pink form. All this with the mixed clematis beyond is a bit overdone: the pink one by itself might be better, or the gorgeous green and white curled one called 'Alba Luxurians' which is hardly ever grown.

Ideas for its use You could fade this into the planting on page 82, with foliage plantings like the one on page 60 near the house. The planting would look good backed by a simple trellis or fence.

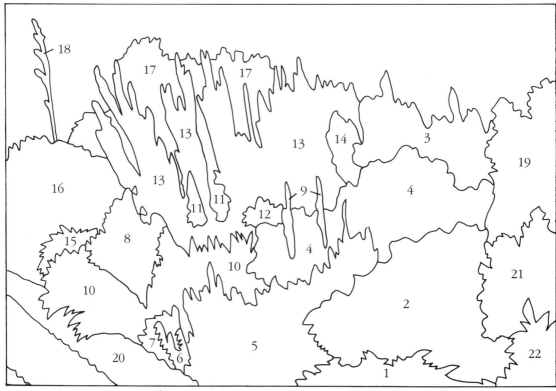

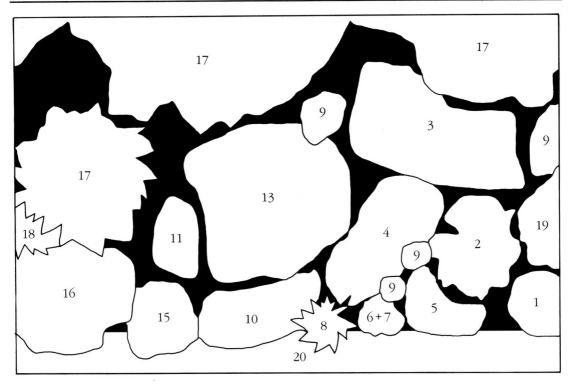

1 *Tradescantia* 'Purple Dome'
2 *Eryngium maritimum*
3 *Aconitum vulgaris* 'Carneum'
4 *Anthemis* 'Powis Sunrise'
5 *Polygonum amplexicaule* 'Inverleith'
6 *Digitalis ambigua*
7 *Penstemon* deep purple form
8 *Eryngium giganteum*
9 *Digitalis purpurea* 'Alba'
10 *Hemerocallis* 'Pink Damask'
11 *Penstemon* 'Sour Grapes'
12 *Lavatera trismestris*
13 *Cimicifuga racemosa*
14 *Penstemon* 'Garnet'
15 *Helleborus orientalis*
16 *Salvia haematodes* 'Indigo'
17 *Clematis* 'Comtesse de Bouchard' and 'Jackmanii'
18 *Phormium tenax* in flower
19 *Acanthus mollis*
20 *Buxus sempervirens*
21 *Cedronella triphylla*
22 *Paeonia lactiflora*

Woodland Gardens

Not all gardens have to be heavily cultivated and highly maintained: a wild woodland garden can also be enjoyable to own, and looks enchanting. Fashionable today, wild gardening especially attracts the 'Greens', modern descendants of the old admirers of the 'Picturesque' now given an important ecological gloss, who want to preserve wildlife, wild flowers, and healthy living. It also attracts gardeners drawn to the hundreds of exquisite plants that can be grown in such situations.

Wild gardens have a long history. Some of the Roman emperors had gardens with contrived wildernesses, and the tradition was revived in Italian gardens during the Renaissance. The idea then spread to other European gardens, and the gardens of the wealthy commonly had 'bosquets', where Nature apparently had free reign. Since the early nineteenth century it has been fashionable, on and off, to garden in orchards, light woodland, and around natural ponds, rather than treating them as purely economic parts of the landscape. During the early Victorian period sophisticated people began to think that the refined 'landscape' gardens of the previous century, all lawns and temples, were too artificial. They rushed, clutching their sketch pads, into the wild countryside, and found that it was beautiful. Of course, they couldn't leave it as it was, especially as there were thousands of marvellous new plants flooding in from abroad that they just had to grow. Consequently, over the rest of the Victorian and early Edwardian period, woodlands became packed with new rhododendrons, Chinese and Indian primulas, skunk cabbages, and Tibetan poppies. Elderly orchard trees, once swathed in wild ivy and a bit of mistletoe, were now wrapped in roses and new species, or hybrids, of clematis and vine. Meadows were decked out with camassias from America, endless new varieties of daffodil, new tulips, and fritillaries from Turkey and Persia. The results, though often entrancing, were really the enthusiasm of a minority of Victorian gardeners. Today, wild gardening is almost a majority interest.

An orchard is packed with potential, and offers the splendid sight of cherries in mid-spring, the foam of myrobalans and damsons even earlier, and the smell (and shades of pink) of all the various apples, let alone the flowers of quince and medlar, and the catkins of hazelnuts. And when the trees could be underplanted with white wild strawberries or the wonderful musk strawberry, wild raspberries, sweet violets, eglantine roses, bluebells and lent lilies, I am always surprised that the country isn't covered with orchard garden after orchard garden.

It is easy to think that 'wild' gardening needs no work, but success is not simply a matter of sowing or planting a few things, and then sitting back while Nature spreads her gorgeous cloak around you. The owner of the sophisticated orchard walk on page 98 goes to considerable effort and expense to achieve the effect, and the owner of the wonderful woodland scene on page 100 is scarcely ever out of the garden, and constantly holds a pair of secateurs to keep things in check and enable right of passage through the jungle. Nevertheless, it is well worth trying if the idea attracts you.

Wildflower seed is easily available (suppliers are listed on page 155), but do not be tempted simply to tear open the packet and drift the seed around you. That's not very effective (we once gathered almost half a pound of white foxglove seed and scattered it about in our tiny piece of woodland so that it would establish there, but not a single plant appeared). It is far better, indeed almost essential, to sow the seeds in trays as if they were more exotic things like antirrhinums, prick out the seedlings when large enough into individual pots or plastic bags, and only plant them out in your grass or under the trees when they are big enough to fend for themselves. The sheets of cowslips on page 98 were treated like this.

If you are planting up a piece of existing woodland, and want something that looks as lovely as the one on page 100, then it is important to take great care of the newly planted things, whether they are undershrubs, herbaceous plants or bulbs, for at least their first year. The trees will all have prior claim to the soil, and will ruthlessly take all the moisture and nutrients they can. Keep checking every few days to see if anything needs watering. We've lost plants because we assumed that, as they were woodlanders, they could look after themselves as soon as they were planted out. Plants need care and attention until they are established, but, once established, vigorous species may well take over the whole area; many of the plants on page 47 are self-sown seedlings.

If you have a blank piece of ground which you want to turn into woodland, then the problems are different. The main one is to stop the rank-growing herbaceous species from starving or even shading out the young trees. For both fruiting and forest trees, we now feed all newly planted trees with liquid fertiliser every week or so for their first couple of seasons. We used just to plant them and forget about them, then wonder why they hardly grew. Though it is possible to grow all your trees from seeds or cuttings (and great fun), it does take much longer than buying them as mature plants. Buy them as large as you can afford, and at least as 'maidens' which are a season or two old, and consist of a single stem, perhaps 1.2–1.5 m (4–5 ft) high.

What you do then depends on the effect you want. Standards (where the plants have a good length of unbranched stem beneath the first main branches) can look fine, especially in groups, but in a small space single multi-stemmed trees look more interesting. If you want such things, cut the maiden's stem at least in half, to encourage three or four side-shoots to sprout, eventually to become trunks in their own right.

If you are planting an orchard, fruit trees are best grown as standards, and if you want the pleasure of being able to walk beneath them, ensure that they are not on dwarfing root-stocks. They can look nice multi-stemmed too, but once the boughs bend beneath the weight of fruit, they become impassable. Give the trees plenty of room – at least 5 m (15 ft) each way, and preferably much more for larger trees like cherries. If you have room for more than two or three, do not treat fruit trees informally as if they were wildlings, but plant them in rows as a 'quincunx', with the trees placed as if they were at the intersections on a piece of graph paper.

If you are fortunate enough to own a piece of old orchard, do not worry if the trees are gnarled, and have not been 'properly' pruned for fifteen, or even fifty, years. Your local 'gaffers' will tell you that they all ought to come out (at least, that's what ours said). If you want a commercial orchard, that might be true. As it is, unpruned and congested, most of your trees will be laden most autumns, and with reasonable quality fruit. You will easily have dozens of times the crop that you can conceivably bottle, jam, freeze, store, and eat direct from the branch. If you do need to overhaul old fruit trees, simply take out a balanced number of whole branches, rather than fiddling around with spurs; a good shaggy-looking tree is the aim. Of course, a well-ordered fruit tree, whether dwarfed, fanned or espaliered against a wall (or a series of taut wires), does look good, too, and can be astonishingly productive. However, even in a tiny garden, a rambling old apple tree can look very romantic, even if every fruit has a maggot.

Sissinghurst has an orchard garden in which the elderly fruits have roses planted to climb into the branches. The idea has become popular, though it does have disadvantages. The fruit becomes tricky to harvest, and when the trees eventually fall over, sawing them up for the fire is even more difficult. Try other things, like clematis, honeysuckles, even celastruses or the decorative vines. There are clematis varieties for almost all year, and, if you don't care for soup plates of colour, some wonderful perfumes too.

Mown paths are useful through the grass, as are seats – even ones built around some of the nicer tree-trunks. A summerhouse is a wonderful addition, too, wreathed in roses if possible (tied to wires stretched over the roof).

Planting 31 A flowery meadow in an orchard

I visited this garden in Northamptonshire on a silvery midday in late April, just after rain. The smell of cow parsley and apple blossom wafted round me, and water glinted on the cowslips and the double pink tulips. The effect was wonderful, and would have been so on almost any day. At one side, out of view, are steps leading down from this grassy terrace, through a tangle of Persian lilacs, to a meadow yellow with primulas. Think, though, before you try to copy it – in this garden, a huge number of old glasshouses is entirely devoted to producing wildflower seedlings in sufficient abundance.

Developments and the seasons Once the main bluebell and daffodil season is over, you could follow it with camassias (mentioned elsewhere in this book, and a much under-used group of bulbs that naturalise well in these conditions), and wild fritillaries, then woodland wild flowers like foxgloves, campions, and, for that wonderful smell of high summer, meadowsweet. After the late summer mow, there won't be much in flower until the following spring, but the fruit will be ripe on the apple trees.

Site Any light woodland would suit this planting, though it does look especially good associated with fruit trees, burgeoning at this time with flower, and making spring a real renaissance. This would make a perfect and easily kept back garden, even in town.

Maintenance and cost The tulips will probably not last more than two years, though you might be surprised. Unless you are very keen to save money, there is not much point in the tiresome business of lifting them each summer: when we bought our

derelict walled garden, a number of varieties that had been engulfed beneath weeds for at least six years were still flowering. Maintenance is only a matter of cutting the grass once the bulbs' leaves have died down, usually some time in June, unless you are lucky enough to have summer wild flowers like campions and scabious, in which case mow in late summer. The mown areas will look unattractive for two or three weeks, until new growth starts, but that is not too high a price to pay for such beauty during the rest of the year.

Props and additions The rustic summerhouse at the end of the mown walk sets the tone perfectly. Almost any sort of rustic shelter would be as good. Seating should be equally primitive.

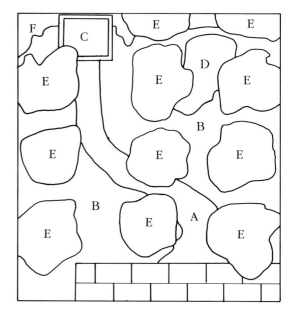

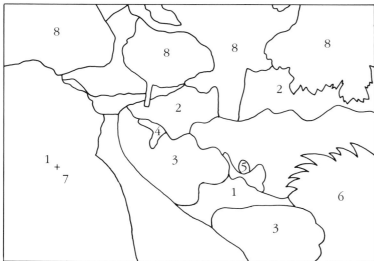

Grassland enriched with:
1 cow parsley (wild species)
2 *Hyacinthoides non-scriptus*
   (bluebell)
3 *Primula veris* (cowslip)
4 *Narcissus poeticus*
5 *Tulipa* 'Peachblossom'
6 *Narcissus* just over
   (try 'Thalia' in soft white)
7 *Leucojum aestivum*
8 Apple, young beech and ash trees

PLAN FOR A SMALL GARDEN
A Mown path
B Meadow planting
C Summerhouse
D Pond
E Fruit trees
F Roses/climbers on back wall

Substitutions The lovely, soft shell-pink of the full double tulip could be replaced by other, similar varieties. 'Pink Triumphator', with its tighter and more formal shape, would be less successful. If you wanted something less sophisticated, try the wild tulip *Tulipa sylvestris* (which should naturalise quite well), or even the stunning little lady tulip (*T. clusiana*), though this would last only a season or two. For the narcissi, you'll need such large quantities of them that it will always be tempting to buy job lots from the local Parks Department. Generally, random mixes look random, not pretty, so choose one or two varieties only – whether good strong-growing yellows like 'King Alfred', or smaller and subtler things like the lent lily (*Narcissus pseudonarcissus*, with charming twisted 'petals'), many of the enchanting 'cyclamineus' hybrids, and almost any of the pheasant's-eye hybrids, most of which have stunning perfume.

Ideas for its use   Gardens like this work well on almost any scale, from fairly generous, as here, to very small. Such a planting would be a solution to weekend cottage gardening, but would make a pleasing vista just attached to a sitting-out area beyond the french windows of any sort of house.

Planting 32   A tapestry of foliage by a shaded path

Almost all John Codrington's plantings in his garden at Stone Cottage consist of a mixture of the most ordinary garden plants, a few more sophisticated things, and plants he has collected on his extensive and exotic travels. This is no exception, giving here a wild, woodlandy look, cunningly put together with strong and interesting foliage – the fatsia and the teazle, for example – mixed with the feathery and the amorphous. Much more exciting than the usual shrubbery.

Development and the seasons   To go with the wild character of this planting, it would be nice to start the season in February with the hanging white and green bells of the snowflake, *Leucojum vernum* (which also has good foliage), followed by white *Anemone blanda* varieties, and perhaps drifts of pale blue scillas or the charming tiny daffodil called *Narcissus asturiensis* (but not both) planted along the front margin. After April the planting as shown would take over.

Site   This is in the fairly deep shade of the surrounding woodland. Transposed, it would work perfectly in a similarly dark urban garden.

Maintenance and cost   Nothing much in the way of costs or difficulty here – though it will help if you are happy to grow things from seed. Little feeding or manuring is necessary, though plenty of thinning and pruning is required. Once the planting is underway, you'll also need to be quite ruthless about taking out excess self-sown seedlings,

especially the teazles, and keeping the elder and rose within bounds. The grand flower stems of the teazle dry well, so harvest them in late September before they have time to drop their seeds.

Props and additions   In a deeply shaded backyard, a formal pool, to bring some sky down into the shadows, would look lovely. Seating might be better in metal than in wood (it is not susceptible to damp), and perhaps painted in deep sea-green.

Substitutions   Euphorbias simpler to find include the wonderful glossy-leaved *Euphorbia robbiae* (its virulently greenish yellow flowers in spring turn bronzy pink later in the season) and the softer *E. polychroma*. Alexanders (*Smyrnium*) is best from seed; it won't germinate unless you leave the pot in which you plant the seed outdoors over the winter, and even then it might take two seasons. Once the

1   *Philadelphus coronarius* 'Aureus' (mock orange)
2   *Prunus laurocerasus* 'Otto Lukyens' (common laurel)
3   *Ferula communis* (giant fennel)
4   *Helleborus foetidus* (stinking hellebore)
5   *Astrantia major* (master wort)
6   *Euphorbia palustris*
7   *Euphorbia* sp.
8   *Petroselinum crispum* 'Hamburgh parsley'
9   *Dipsacus fullonum* (teazle)
10   *Rosa* 'Moyesii'
11   *Fatsia japonica*
12   *Lunaria annua* seedlings (honesty)
13   *Smyrnium perfoliatum* (alexanders)
14   *Sambucus niger* (elder)
15   *Garrya elliptica*

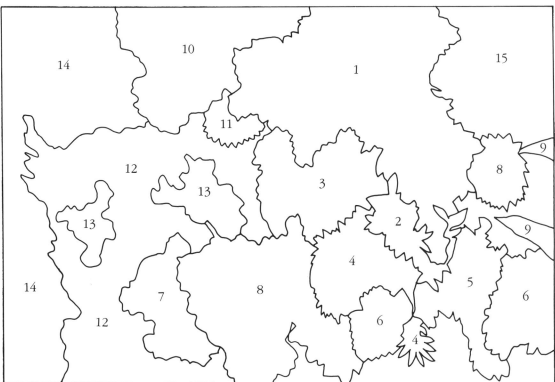

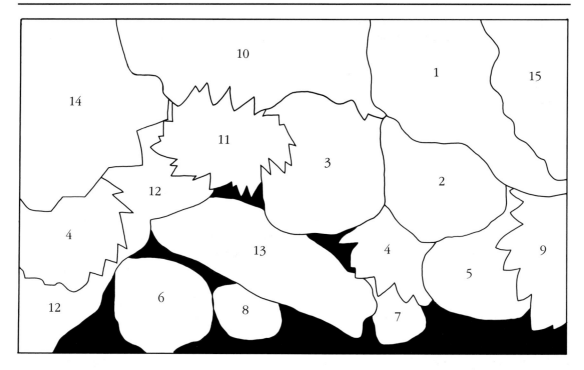

1 *Philadelphus coronarius* 'Aureus' (mock orange)
2 *Prunus laurocerasus* 'Otto Lukyens' (common
   laurel)
3 *Ferula communis* (giant fennel)
4 *Helleborus foetidus* (stinking hellebore)
5 *Astrantia major* (master wort)
6 *Euphorbia palustris*
7 *Euphorbia* sp.
8 *Petroselinum crispum* 'Hamburgh parsley'
9 *Dipsacus fullonum* (teazle)
10 *Rosa* 'Moyesii'
11 *Fatsia japonica*
12 *Lunaria annua* seedlings (honesty)
13 *Smyrnium perfoliatum* (alexanders)
14 *Sambucus niger* (elder)
15 *Garrya elliptica*

seedlings are established in the open ground, they
naturalise well, and the young jade-green flower
stems are well worth having. A good rose would be
'Anne of Gierstane', a briar-like pink single, though
you might also like to try the ancient 'Alba Maxima',
a shrub that will also climb, with double white
flowers that smell ravishing.

Ideas for its use   This would make a pretty backyard in a shaded site. Here it borders a roughish
lawn, but it might be even better around a stone or
brick patio, where the philadelphus and roses in
flower could be enjoyed on summer evenings.

Pools and Ponds

Gardeners have always been fascinated by water in the garden, from the time of the first cities of Sumer and Ur to the present day, with the current vogue for moulded fibreglass pondlets. Almost all the water shown in these pages is pure artifice, from the fine courtyard pool on page 108 to the marvellously natural-seeming pond on page 106, created from an old farm courtyard that filled with water when cleared of rubbish (the owners, at first horrified, then delighted, exploited the planting opportunity with relish and style). Even in a dry garden on a raised beach, water 'features' can be made from galvanised iron water tanks (a nice formal design, and deep enough to keep fish happy, though no fun if you have small children), cast-iron dough bins, even old air-raid shelters. Even moulded fibreglass ponds can be used successfully. Few good ones seem to be made from plastic sheeting; the edges are almost always difficult to disguise unless you use expensive masonry or brick edging and detailing.

If you like moving water and fountains, or have to have a lion or satyr mask spouting into your pool (a simple spigot of lead looks just as authentic, unless you have a garden of Italian grandeur), ensure that the pumping mechanism is far enough away not to drown out the sound of plashing water. Since masks are supposed to be outlets of springs, it helps if they look as if they might just be that. The water looks best, too, if it falls into a formal pool or square tank. In the courtyard on page 39 the vertical water jet falls back on a flat square of stone, and makes an entirely admirable noise. Motors big enough to provide rivulets and waterfalls don't seem to give rise to elegant gardening.

One of the nicest examples of a pool, not shown in this book, is also one of the simplest: a square sheet of water set in a lawn flanked by yew hedges, and with a grand seat on one side. It has no fountain, no stone margin (though these can look lovely with a suitable array of pots), and no planting. The water simply reflects the sky.

Planting 33　Wild waterside elegance under trees

This intriguing pool, from John Codrington's intriguing garden in Hambleton, Rutland, looks like pure jungle, and yet a path around it is carefully routed to give elegant glimpses of water through the vegetation, and to take you to the water's edge where the view is particularly good. This luscious planting depends mainly on the contrast between linear foliage (the irises), big, broad leaves (the heracleum and the skunk cabbages) and the shrub planting on the far side of the water. There are also native ferns nearby, and duckweed on the water to add to the variety of greenery. Moorhens and ducks will enjoy this pool, as will local frogs and newts. You'll need some fish to keep the mosquito population under control. As in the rest of the garden, the plants are a mixture of natives and sophisticated garden species.

Developments and the seasons　The image is so soft and natural that any bright spring colour would look out of place. The unfurling fronds of nearby ferns would give emerald green, and perhaps the wonderful ever-flowering forget-me-not for damp places (*Myosotis scorpioides* 'Mermaid') could be used to give an early haze of blue. Late in the year, the yellows and browns of autumn in the low light, will look lovely. You could add some climbers, like *Clematis flammula* and *C. fargesii* for perfume and seed heads (the latter species, even later flowering than the other, smells of primroses).

Site　Without the woodland behind it (giving shelter, privacy and shade), the effect would be vastly reduced; this is therefore a pond for an overgrown part of the garden, or beneath a canopy of trees. If the woodland is dull, add balsam poplar, aspens and silver willows. Alternatively, if you would like something to crop, make a copse of hazels and sloes (wonderful in flower in spring) with this pond at its core. With such steep banks as this, the pool could be made with butyl sheeting, a material not eschewed by the owner elsewhere in the garden.

Maintenance and cost　In spite of its look of simplicity, this planting takes quite a lot of maintenance to keep it as elegantly controlled as this. Even though you'll spend the first four or five years wanting everything to grow as fast as possible, once it has you'll find it impenetrable: the planting round this pond is edited almost every day.

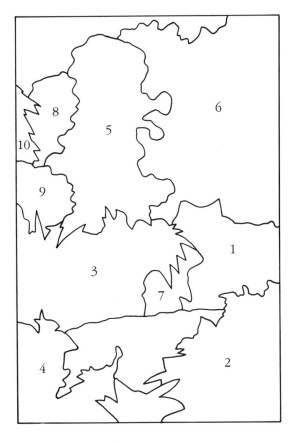

1　*Iris pseudacorus* (yellow flag iris)
2　*Iris kaempferi*
3　*Iris pseudacorus* 'Bastardii'
4　*Ligularia* 'Greynog Gold'
5　*Heracleum mantegazzianum* (giant hogweed)
6　*Spirea thunbergii*
7　*Lysichiton americanus* (skunk cabbage)
8　*Taxus baccata* 'Fastigiata'
9　*Solidago* 'Goldenmosa'
10　*Arundinaria anceps*

Props and additions   The pool is kidney shaped; an islet might look rather over-elaborate, but a plank bridge across one arm of the pool might look fetching, perhaps with the railings swathed with honeysuckle or roses. A modest shed or pavilion in which to sit and enjoy the view might also be a useful addition.

Substitutions   Not everyone, especially if there are children, will want giant hogweed, and so this could go.

Ideas for its use   This is not really suitable for a small urban garden, but perfect for an unused part of something larger. It could easily make use of other people's trees (say, in a neighbour's garden).

Planting 34 Lush bog plants for a tiny garden

This painter's garden, behind a small cottage high in the Pentland hills near Edinburgh, is packed with plants and detail. Through imagination and clever planting, a tiny pool, created from a dull fibreglass garden-centre pond, has been transformed into something original and delightful.

Development and the seasons   The marsh marigold is the first plant to flower, in about April, after which the whole planting gives a variety of soft yellows, pale purples and sharp pink (and perfume with *Primula alpicola*), and finishes in the early autumn with the amethyst bells of the hosta flowers and the bronzing foliage of the ferns. Over winter, the dead foliage will look handsome here, especially edged with frost.

1 *Osmunda regalis* (royal fern)
2 *Primula alpicola*
3 *Hosta* 'Thomas Hogg'
4 *Dryopteris filix-mas* (male fern)
5 *Milium effusum* 'Bowles Golden'
6 *Iris pseudacorus* 'Bastardii' (yellow flag iris)
7 *Menyanthes trifoliata* (wild bog bean)
8 *Caltha palustris* (marsh marigold)
9 *Primula* candelabra seedling

Site This heavily disguised fibreglass pool, wedged into a sloping garden, gets plenty of light but freezes solid in winter. Farther south, its small size and luscious planting mean that it would need constant checking to ensure that it didn't dry out. It would also tolerate more shade, and would be an easy addition to a small patio. (It is surrounded here by lavish and pretty plantings of meconopsis, rhododendrons and roses.)

Maintenance and cost The bog bean and the grass (*Milium*) need watching carefully if they are not to take over the planting, though everything else is fairly restrained. After a couple of years, discreet thinning will be necessary each spring.

Props and additions This garden rises directly from a paved yard, and is the whole view from the seats there and the studio. Seating is extremely simple, while elsewhere in the garden, fragments of grand garden decoration appear through the vegetation. Pots need too much attention for the owner to keep here, but if you had time to look after them, big glazed pots filled with more bog plants – say the marvellous orange-scarlet *Lobelia cardinalis* or the soft orange or burgundy forms of *Mimulus glutinosus* – would go prettily with this planting.

Substitutions Everything here is easy to get hold of, except perhaps the wild bog bean (menyanthes), which has wonderfully scented flowers. You should avoid digging it up from the wild, but try some of the wild-flower specialist nurseries. Instead of the pale yellow wild flag iris, you might find that the variegated form makes more impact (though the flowers are a more solid yellow, and less exciting). Almost any medium-sized hosta would do, but avoid anything likely to swamp the whole planting, such as the potentially vast *Hosta sieboldiana*.

Ideas for its use This would be perfect beside the patio in a tiny back garden, or at the side of a shrubbery in a slightly larger one. It would even bear the addition of a faucet or a half-obscured mask of a satyr, spouting water.

Planting 35 Rustic sophistication by a farmhouse duckpond

Less brave souls, finding a spring in their front yard, would have dug a culvert and kept the yard for parking. Mirabel Osler and her husband decided instead to turn almost the entire yard, flanked on three sides by walls, outbuildings and house, into a pond. The result is a triumph. The irregular shape of this almost natural pool allows generous planting areas, paths, and enchanting views both to and from the house itself. The planting itself, using fairly simple things, works wonderfully.

Developments and the seasons Since water holds its interest through the winter (as does the light that it reflects), you don't need too much colour too early; in any case, the marsh marigolds will be flowering in April, and the whole garden

1 *Nymphaea* unknown pink hybrid
2 *Iris pseudacorus* (yellow flag iris)
3 *Dryopteris filix-mas* (male fern)
4 *Digitalis purpurea* (foxglove)
5 *Hedera helix* (common ivy)
6 *Campanula porscharskyana* (bellflower)
7 *Aquilegia* pale pink form (columbine)
8 *Rosa glauca* (shrub rose) *Meconopsis cambrica* (Welsh poppy) behind it (8a on plan)
9 *Caltha palustris* (marsh marigold)
10 *Geranium endressii* (crane's-bill)
11 *Mimulus guttatus*
12 *Primula* candelabra seedlings
13 *Iris kaempferi* (beardless iris)
14 *Rosa* 'New Dawn' (climbing rose)
15 *Geranium magnificum* (crane's-bill)
16 *Iris sibirica*
17 *Iris japonica* (crested iris)

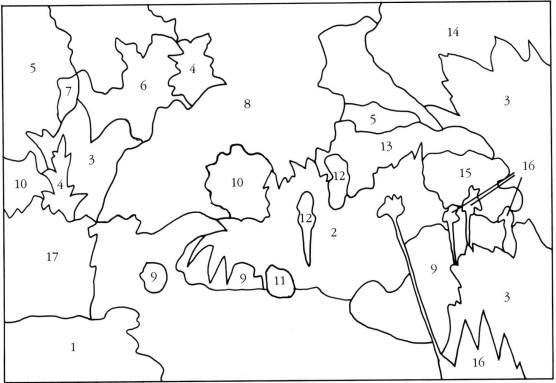

soon follows. Out of view is a nice old copper filled with flowers; a sprawl of palest yellow tulips (perhaps the elegant native *Tulipa sylvestris*) would look nice in spring, followed by white perennial or East Lothian stocks for summer (though the perfume might be a bit over-oriental).

Site This pond, excavated from an old farmhouse yard, gets plenty of sun, though nothing here would fail if it were much more shaded. A smaller, plastic-sided pool could work almost as prettily, as long as the surrounding soil was kept fairly moist. Away from the water's edge, the plants here will all succeed under ordinary garden conditions.

Maintenance and cost Basic planting costs are low, and the time taken to establish the plants is short: the roses would look good three or four seasons after planting, by which time the herbaceous species will need thinning. Maintenance of the water surface is important (it needs to be clear), and the more inelegant weeds will have to be removed from the margins.

Props and additions This is so rustic and refreshing that seating could be just a low bench of mown turf, suitably cushioned after a rainy spell. Otherwise, use local stone to make benches, or just bench ends. Green or blue cast-iron seats would

1 *Nymphaea* unknown pink hybrid
2 *Iris pseudacorus* (yellow flag iris)
3 *Dryopteris filix-mas* (male fern)
4 *Digitalis purpurea* (foxglove)
5 *Hedera helix* (common ivy)
6 *Campanula porscharskyana* (bellflower)
7 *Aquilegia* pale pink form (columbine)
8 *Rosa glauca* (shrub rose) *Meconopsis cambrica* (Welsh poppy) behind it (8a on plan)

9 *Caltha palustris* (marsh marigold)
10 *Geranium endressii* (crane's-bill)
11 *Mimulus guttatus*
12 *Primula* candelabra seedlings
13 *Iris kaempferi* (beardless iris)
14 *Rosa* 'New Dawn' (climbing rose)
15 *Geranium magnificum* (crane's-bill)
16 *Iris sibirica*
17 *Iris japonica* (crested iris)

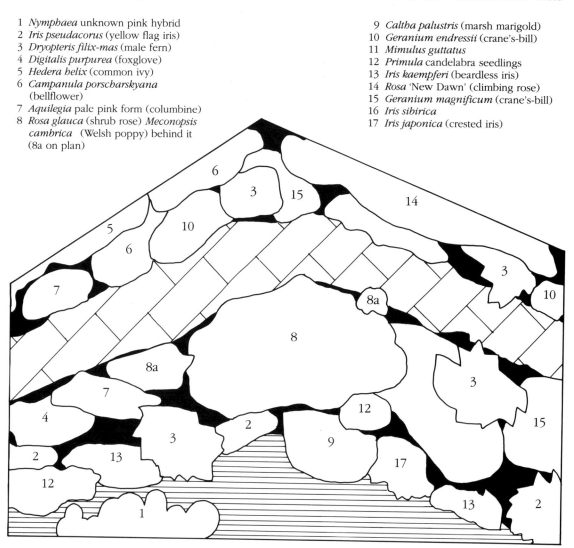

also work well. Here, stone steps ascending to the front porch are lined with pots and cans of geraniums, and make a perfect place to sit.

Substitutions Obviously, this is a fairly flexible planting, and the lovelier for that. No other shrub rose is quite like this one (it will be hung with brick-red berries by October), though other shrub roses might look almost as good; try either the more usual red *Rosa* 'Moyesii', or even *R.* 'Cantabrigensis', for its brief but heavy showers of soft yellow flowers. Against the back wall, rather than a glossy-leaved rose, a vast half-species might look good: perhaps 'The Garland', or still bigger 'Paul's Himalayan Musk' or 'Sander's White'. For something to spark the blue irises, add some of the several lovely white forms of *Iris sibirica*.

Ideas for its use This would be a difficult look to achieve in a city, and it would not look right in the country unless it were stony too. But the planting would work as well on a sloping soil bank as on these delectable stone sides – and be far better than using the sort of imported stone sold for rockeries.

Planting 36 A luscious arrangement round a small pond

Few gardeners have enough space or time to create large and enticing sheets of water. This planting at Tan Cottage, shown here in late June, is an object lesson in how to make maximum use of a tiny pond (here in a front garden), with interesting plants that make perfect use of the damp conditions and the reflectivity of the water. The owners spend much of their time gardening, which accounts for the sharp maintenance; you could let yours get a little more shaggy than this before the stork vanished behind the jungle.

Developments and the seasons The planting is splendidly balanced as it is, and something nice should be happening for most of the season. Even in deep winter it will look interesting, with the bare branches of the maple and the stork giving an oriental look to the scene.

Site This garden is fairly heavily shaded, although, with enough moisture, everything here would do well in full sun – and the pot plants (18 and 19) would flower better too. High light levels may make the pond somewhat greener, and you may have to scoop out the duckweed.

Maintenance and cost Planting and other costs are negligible compared to the initial cost of building the pool and finding its decorations. The irises will need to have their dead foliage cut away in autumn, but little else needs to be done other than general tidying. Real herons may gulp down any fish you add.

Props and additions The bird sculpture helps to give structure to the pond in the depths of winter, though you might prefer to let the plantings do that. You could add some pots of the elegant *Francoa ramosa*, with spines of white and pink flowers (one of Gertrude Jekyll's favourite waterside plants). In a tiny garden, have a nice seat by the water's edge, and preferably where you can see its reflection from the house.

Substitutions This complex little poolside planting (owned, needless to say, by an enthusiastic plant collector), may need a few substitutions. If you can't get hold of the grand scirpus by the heron, then use the variegated form of *Iris pseudacorus*, which isn't quite as grand, but will give you handsome yellow flowers. Instead of the gold-leaved sagina, you might like to try the easier-to-find *Lysimachia nummularia* 'Aurea', which will relish the same situation and look almost as pretty. Many Japanese maples would look good here; if you want one without the purplish leaves of 'Atropurpurea', then try the delectable *Acer palmatum* 'Aureum'.

The planting could also possibly be simplified without losing too much of its character. The pots holding the felicia and the osteospermum might be better placed near where you will sit (there are hardy osteospermums that you could use by the pool), in which case let the golden filipendula take up the space. Even better, this planting sometimes has the graceful 'Bowles Golden' grass (a variety of *Milium effusum*) allowed to grow amongst it. It does wonderfully in wet conditions like these, and is almost worth building a pool for.

Ideas for its use The planting detail is so dense that it would work on a patio too, even right against

living-room windows, from which you could appreciate leaves and flowers for most of the day.

 1 *Arrhenatherum bulbosus* 'Variegata'
 2 *Alchemilla mollis* (lady's mantle)
 3 *Filipendula ulmaria* 'Aurea' (meadowsweet)
 4 *Hosta sieboldiana*
 5 *Polypodium vulgare* (polypody)
 6 *Penstemon* 'Glabra'
 7 *Iris pallida* 'Variegata' (yellow flag iris)
 8 *Filipendula ulmaria* 'Variegata' (meadowsweet)
 9 *Acer palmatum* 'Atropurpurea' (maple)
10 *Osteospermum jucundum*
11 *Arabis albida* 'Variegata'
12 *Rhododendron* bright pink variety
13 *Pulsatilla alpina*
14 *Scirpus tabernaemontani* 'Albescens'
15 *Miscanthus zebrinus*
16 *Nymphaea* 'Mrs Richmond'
17 *Cimicifuga* seedling (bug bane)
18 *Felicia amelloides* 'Variegata'
19 *Osteospermum jucundum* 'Notcutts form'
20 *Onoclea sensibilis*
21 *Sagina pilifera* 'Aurea'

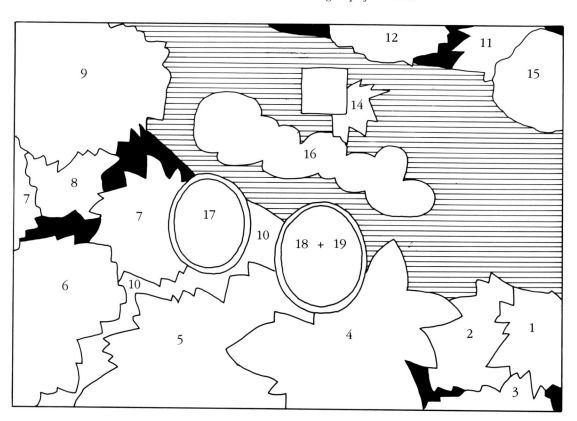

Parterres

As in Victorian times, there is today a divergence of gardening ideals. While some gardeners hanker after the half wild but pretty, where the shears and the spray gun are never seen, others long for the ultimate in artifice and elaboration (naturally, greedy gardeners want both). The parterre, meaning almost any horizontal 'pattern' garden, can satisfy either taste: it can be either informally pretty or grandly formal. Parterres, once again fashionable, have been made at least since the gardens of ancient Greece, and only went out of vogue during the enthusiasm for landscape gardens of the eighteenth century.

The pattern of a parterre can be created from grass, gravel or even sand, with some sort of low hedging (thrift, lavender, box, santolina and rosemary can all be used for this), to emphasise the design and to keep everything in place. The parterre can be used to display roses, herbs, culinary plants, or plantings designed to recapture the look of historic periods (whether medieval or 'Queen Anne'). Electric hedge trimmers, mowers and edgers greatly reduce the expense of their upkeep, and using chemical weedkillers makes the maintenance of gravel paths easy. They're remarkably exciting things to make, if expensive. The final effect usually looks best if the ground is reasonably horizontal. If you do need to do some levelling over anything more than a few square metres, it might be worth hiring a mini-bulldozer for the coarse work. The final levelling will almost certainly need to be done by hand. Make your design on graph and tracing paper and transfer it to the bare ground with builders' line stretched taut between pegs.

The 'garden history' movement is helping the new interest in parterres to become established. Fired by the desire for authentic gardens as much as house interiors and furnishings, many people are starting to make the sort of gardens that might once have graced their houses. Nonetheless, if you like the idea of a parterre then have one, even if you don't have the right sort of house. Most of the 'Art History' parterres have inaccuracies, either in the props, the plants, or even the settings themselves. One of the most charming parterres I've seen (too young to show here, alas) is sandwiched between the sleepers of a railway line and a British Rail fence.

The historically minded will discover that there were once many types of parterre, such as 'closed' and 'open' knots ('closed' knots, like the one in front of the Old Palace at Hatfield, or in the Tradescant Trust's garden at Lambeth, look good from a distance, but you can't actually get into them to look at the plants). Most of the others are better for the general gardener; one of the reasons for dividing up a small space into myriad paths is (and no doubt was) that it provides a good way of displaying many different plants in a small space.

A parterre does not need to be taken too seriously: it can be made for sheer enjoyment, and filled with lovely flowers. Though none of the beds should be deeper than about 1 m (3-4 ft) so that you can weed or crop them without having to stand inside the planting space, try not to make the plan too big or too complicated. Though parterres can be used for 'conspicuous consumption' (and were certainly so used in the past), modern ones always look better if they are simply designed for inconspicuous delight instead.

114

Planting 37 Grand designs and simple plantings achieve perfection

Though this garden at Levens Hall in Cumbria is most famous for its extraordinary topiary yews, much else repays a close look. The Victorian parterres have a delightful balance between the weight of the box hedges and the plant fillings. The fillings themselves make use of all sorts of things, ancient and modern, handled in good broad plantings in interesting colours, demonstrating that the bedding flora can be vastly more fun than the usual range of lobelias, alyssum and scarlet salvia.

Developments and the seasons If you want to add spring bedding, and keep a comparable colour scheme, the only green-flowered bulbs to match the lovely little nicotiana are green-streaked tulips (often listed in catalogues as 'viridifloras'), or some of the parrot tulips which have fringed petals. If not, you could also use hyacinths, or copy an idea at Hidcote, where a sheet of *Scilla sibirica* bulbs is left permanently in the ground, beneath fuchsia bushes pruned each autumn back to the stools. Here, the scilla's bulbs would be disturbed when planting annuals, but they could be left beneath the diascias. Other beds could contain tough bulbs like ornithogalums and muscari, all of which almost relish some disturbance (once in, they will be there for ever). If you want a green summer-flowering bulb, look for the jade-green *Galtonia princeps*, which is easy to grow from seed.

Site This planting is in a fairly cold garden, with a reasonable amount of shade, but everything would succeed in deeper shade still.

Maintenance and cost The diascias will soon spread once you have a few plants, if you divide them every two months or so. The flowers cut well.

The nicotiana seeds abundantly, though you will need to collect a few pods since the seeds don't always overwinter outdoors. It also makes an excellent pot plant. You might want to omit the dahlias and, for a more interesting splash of brilliance, use *Salvia grahamii*, ethereal but thrillingly scarlet.

Props and additions The atmosphere in this part of the garden is restrained; any props need to reinforce this. A seat under the ginkgo tree (the leaves turn a pleasing yellow in autumn), would look good painted either ochre or Chinese red. The scene could do with some big containers holding vast sprawls of marguerites (either yellow 'Jamaica Primrose' or soft pink 'Vancouver'), pale pink lilies or grand foliage. Stonework and statuary might be more than is needed, though a water tank edged with box, like a mirror set in the garden, would be a good addition.

Substitutions The slightly ethereal charm of this planting is most attractive, but you could easily increase the intensity of the colour by using the green form of *Nicotiana affinis* (the species used here has distinctive turquoise anthers but no perfume), and many things would give a heavier blue – try the annual *Phacelia campanularia*. There are many new diascias, a number with more electric pinks than the one here, such as *Diascia vigilis*.

Ideas for its use With electric hedge cutters, gardens like this are now easier to maintain than at any time in the last fifty years. This elegant parterre needs some space, but would look good between a small lawn and an orchard planting (like the one on page 98).

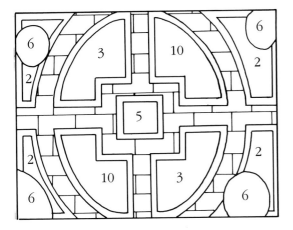

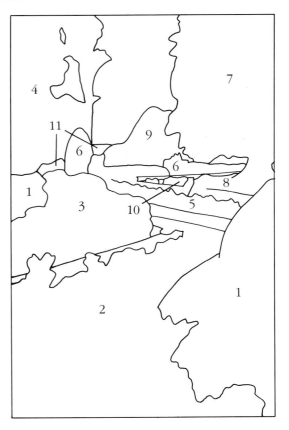

1 *Buxus sempervirens* (common box)
2 *Myosotis alpestris* (forget-me-not)
3 *Nicotiana langsdorfii* (tobacco plant)
4 *Taxodium distichum* (bald cyress)
5 *Diascia rigescens* 'Ruby Field'
6 *Taxus baccata* 'Aurea' (golde yew)
7 *Ginkgo biloba* (maidenhair tree)
8 *Galeobdolon luteum* (yellow archangel)
9 *Taxus baccata* (common yew)
10 *Felicia amelloides* 'Variegata' (blue marguerite)
11 Dahlias mixed

Planting 38 Fragrant enchantment in the
grand manner

This remarkable and arresting parterre in the grand manner is at Broughton Castle in Oxfordshire. It is enclosed by ancient walls which hold in the perfume of box, roses, and the wonderful dianthus, seen here in July. The box edges have an intriguing section, sloping outwards from their roots to make enclosures shaped like pie pans. Though built on a generous scale, the parterre is not complex and would be almost equally enchanting cut down to suit a much smaller garden.

Developments and the seasons From early summer when the roses and pinks start to flower there's plenty happening until late-October or so, when the first frosts slow things down. For some colour in early spring, copy the Hidcote idea on page 115 – though try the tough and palest blue *Scilla tubergeniana* instead.

Site This planting is in a large, open, sunny courtyard, but would be equally possible in something smaller and a little less sunny.

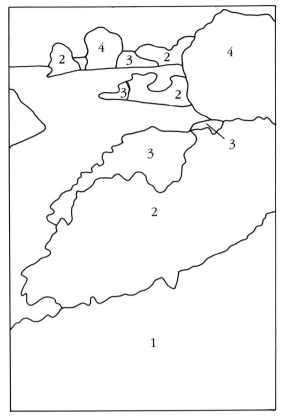

1 *Buxus sempervirens* (common box)
2 *Rosa* 'Gruss an Aachen'
3 *Dianthus* 'Rainbow Loveliness' (pink)
4 *Salix lanata* (woolly willow)

Maintenance and cost There is little maintenance apart from pruning the roses to keep them in scale, trimming the box two or three times a year and some general weeding. The dianthus is short-lived and you will need new young plants each spring ready to replace those that have failed. Seed is easily saved, and it also self-sows plentifully. The flowers smell wonderful: spicy and fruity at the same time, and very strong.

Props and additions This planting, charming as it is, is fairly luscious; match it with your seating. Here, a centrepiece is provided by an extraordinary Victorian cast-iron urn, like an elaborate mushroom with the gills only, and no cap. A simple sundial would be as effective. If you used a small rose for the 'filling', a central standard tree would be fun. Use either another rose, like 'Ballerina' used elsewhere in this lovely garden, a bay or a dark-leaved privet (some interesting species, neatly pruned, appear in London garden centres; elsewhere, make your own).

Substitutions Some people dislike the smell of box; others object to it because it holds snails. Many other shrubs could be used for edgings like this one, clipped into the unusual 'tart mould' shape. Some rosemary varieties are easily tonsured (the white-flowered sort is especially good), and if you fancied a silver-grey hedge, use *Santolina chamaecyparissus*. Other good roses to use would be 'Baroness Rothschild' or 'Nymphenburg', or even hard-pruned ramblers like the lovely 'Blush Noisette', or the pink-clustered 'Old Blush Monthly', still flowering here in October. Most of the 'old roses', lovely though many of them are, have too short a season for this sort of planting in a small garden.

Ideas for its use This would make an amusing front garden with a box-edged outer planting, perhaps like the one on page 121, or the one from another part of this same garden on page 80.

Planting 39 Stone and evergreens make a garden for all seasons

Parterres are about patterns, and here is one (at Moseley Old Hall, near Wolverhampton) where the pattern is all: in this rather severe garden, the plants are reduced to architecture. Such things are more common in France and Holland, though this formal planting would perfectly suit some British and American houses too. This restrained scheme mostly in gravels and box, though not a garden to bowl you over with the delights of spring, has a strong atmosphere of stillness. It looks wonderful in deepest winter and, in a small private garden, could be lavishly decorated with pots of flowers and elegant seats.

Developments and the seasons The point of this planting is that it looks almost the same all year round. If you wanted seasons you could alter the arbour planting round the perimeter, or add big square tubs of flowers beside the arbour. Alternatively, use citrus standards in tubs instead of the standard box trees. For a good crop of hazelnuts, plant several varieties. The nuts are delicious fresh from the tree, and will keep well into the New Year.

Site Box survives in such deep shade that parterres like this can be found in the shadiest courtyards of Europe; it would do well in such a place if you have one.

Maintenance and cost If you don't mind using chemical weedkillers on the gravel (the coarse one here should perhaps be finer), the only work will be box clipping and raking the gravel paths to keep them free of footprints. Autumn leaves will be a minor nuisance.

Props and additions The whole garden is a 'prop' in effect, so choose additions carefully. It is a garden for walking through rather than sitting in: the nut walk and the tunnel are both extremely pretty inside, and a delight to use. A central fountain or square pool would be a charming addition.

1 *Buxus sempervirens* (common box)
2 *Buxus* standards (box)
3 *Vitis vinifera* 'Purpurea' (grape vine)
4 *Lavandula* 'Hidcote' (lavender)
5 *Corylus avellana* (hazel)
6 *Carpinus betulus* (hornbeam)

Substitutions If you find the dark green of the box hedge too harsh, hyssop would give a slightly softer look, and you could let it flower in late summer, before trimming it in autumn. A parterre of santolina can also look stunning, with a warmer shade of gravel. For a slight contrast with the edging, you could use standard hollies or, in good light, standard bays instead of the box standards. I find the purple-leaved grape a bit heavy-looking with the deep purple lavender; better here might be the taller and more heavily scented 'Old English' lavender, or you might even prefer the lovely white- or pink-flowered forms. Instead of the purple grape (the leaves, though, go bronze and scarlet in autumn), it might be fun to use instead the silvery green 'Dusty Miller' grape (sometimes under the name 'Incana'), combined with strands of delicious musk rose and honeysuckle. The delightful nut walk at the back could be underplanted with a few bluebells and lent lilies.

Ideas for its use   This National Trust planting is attached to a famous but quite modest house, and is probably more suitable for a grander site than here. Since it is a piece of display rather than a place in which to linger, it would be best in a front garden or courtyard of a suitable town house, or a glamorous country mansion. If you crammed the beds with flowers, however (perhaps the enchanting mix on page 80), it would work anywhere.

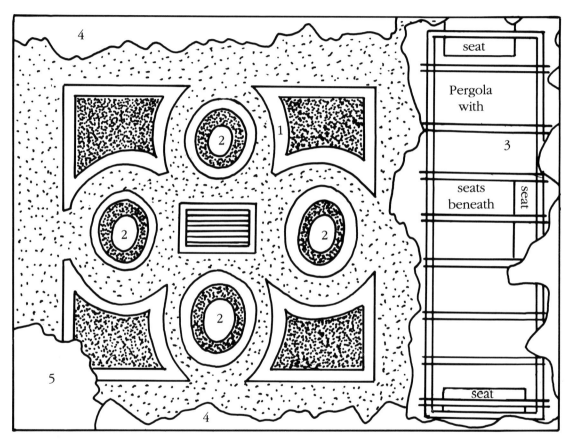

1 *Buxus sempervirens* (common box)
2 *Buxus* standards (box)
3 *Vitis vinifera* 'Purpurea' (grape vine)
4 *Lavandula* 'Hidcote' (lavender)
5 *Corylus avellana* (hazel)
6 *Carpinus betulus* (hornbeam)

Slopes, Steps and Walls

Slopes, steps and walls in a garden can all present exciting opportunities for perfect plantings, although they can also pose more problems than gardening on one level. If your garden is on a slope, it is possible to hire a bulldozer (or mini-dozer for a small space) to terrace it as you please. If you split your sloping garden into several different levels, separated by low terraces, you could plant hedges on the slope. It is much cheaper than building retaining walls or having grand balustrades of reconstituted stone. Failing hedges, you could use one of the dense ground-cover roses, though they can be dull, and need a lot of maintenance. You might prefer a show like that on page 130, where delectable and dense planting keeps down weeds and consolidates the soil. With such a planting, you get the best of both worlds.

Very high or steep slopes will need steps of some sort, whether these are made of stone or just baulks of timber pegged into the slope and back-filled with soil or gravel. Planting steps can be great fun, using things like the tiny and delicious Corsican mint, some of the lovely little erigerons, pink and tenacious, or real pinks like the native *Dianthus gratianopolitanus* (Cheddar pink), ferns, sedums, houseleeks, or the ferny leaves and soft yellow flowers of something like *Corydalis cheilanthifolia*. At the sides of steps, real ferns mixed with day lilies look especially good.

Steps should not be more than 15 cm (6 in) high, 11 cm (4½ in) for grand elegance. They give marvellous sites for props, whether for seats at the top or bottom, or for lots and lots of pots and tubs.

Steps look good coming up through gateways, under trees and down into courtyards, and offer tremendous opportunities for romance and drama (and, of course, expense).

Steep slopes and steps can often be associated with walls, boundaries and fences. In small gardens or enclosed parts of larger ones (like courtyards and patios, or that odd area between the garage and the house), boundaries are very visible but there is no reason why they should imprison you without looking wonderful, or at least making a good background to the rest of the garden.

Climbers of all sorts can add immeasurably to the pleasures of all gardens, and they are lovely plants to grow. You can quite cheaply create privacy in your garden by simply enclosing it with netting or trellis, and covering it with twining climbers. Most such species need a trellis or stretched wires against a wall or fence in order to be able to climb it. A few climbers will climb by themselves (their built-in support systems are sticky-tipped tendrils or short clinging roots sprouting along the stems). If you don't want to go to the trouble of wiring or trellising a wall, then put up ivy, a self-clinger that doesn't lose its leaves in the winter. The leaf stalks can offer a foothold to other twining climbers that need support. Once the ivy is established, wind the other things through it (clematis, in its myriad forms, can look particularly lovely like this).

In the wild, few climbers have space entirely to themselves, though wild ivy often does. It is more natural and common to find a mix of honeysuckles, vines, clematis, and so on, and this can look wonderful copied in the garden; rather than space your climbers along the wall (a rose, a jasmine, a vine, and then another rose), pile them on top of one another. When planting such things, match the plants to the scale. For example, if you put *Rosa filipes* 'Kiftsgate' up a suburban fence, the suburb itself will disappear beneath the thorns, and the rose 'Paul's Himalayan Musk' up a dwarf fruit tree will soon smother it. Even *Clematis montana* from the garden centre will happily go up a three-storey house, and a good way down the other side.

If you want quick effects, a number of annual creepers are worth using. If you live somewhere warm, all the morning glories are worth a try (and can become a weed in really warm gardens), though the canary creeper *Tropaeolum peregrinum* (see page 133) is a charmer, and even *Cobaea scandens* (cathedral bells) can look stunning. There is also a good variegated annual hop (but avoid the ordinary one which is a perennial thug, and glamorous only in fruit; although the dried cones can be used in swags or bunches). At the end of the season, tear the foliage from the support. The perennial golden-leaved hop is in a different category, and can look wonderful. In the garden at Vann (page 20), it is mixed with white wisteria, and the two plants ascend behind a vast greeny blue-leaved *Euphorbia characias*. The combination is stunning.

Putting netting or wires up a large expanse of wall can be expensive (you will need 'vine eyes' and stretchers to do it properly), and there is no cheaper method, for the weight of a mature climber can be quite substantial. The main disadvantage created by wall plants is the difficulty of maintaining the structure beneath, especially that of a house. Painting, pointing and other maintenance become difficult, and the self-clinging climbers can damage the fabric of walls. Ivies, for instance, do sometimes put proper roots right into damp and poorly maintained stonework, and as these expand as the plant grows, the plant can cause serious damage. Virginia creepers cling with great enthusiasm and, if torn off, will leave the little pads of 'glue' stuck to the wall. Don't let climbers near gutters or roof tiles. (Even clematis may twine between tiles, and can be difficult to remove.)

Planting 40 Elegant simplicity for a wall or fence

It is sometimes the small corners of a garden, however big that garden might be, which show the owner's skill at putting plants together. This astonishingly simple mix of simple things at Great Dixter in Sussex works extremely well, and would look almost as good against concrete as it does here against a sixteenth-century wall.

Developments and the seasons   The season starts in March with the euphorbia, and finishes with the rows of scarlet berries on the cotoneaster in early winter, so almost nothing more is needed.

Site   This planting, elegant as it is, would suit almost any wall, ancient or modern. It would tolerate sun, but would prefer partial shade.

Maintenance and cost   This scheme costs almost nothing. Gardening friends will almost certainly have seedlings of the cotoneaster, and a few spare sprigs of periwinkle. The garden is easy from seed, too. Maintenance consists of stopping the euphorbia and the periwinkle invading the lawn and securing the cotoneaster to the wall; tie it to occasional nails, rather than going to the expense of putting up wires. The gentian is fairly easily grown from seed, and should be in flower by its second season. The usual blue is gorgeous, much better than the rarer pale blue and white forms.

Props and additions   You could perhaps add an ivy behind the cotoneaster, to give contrast to the small-scale leaves of that plant. If you wanted yet more, another addition could be one of the less vigorous clematis species, possibly *Clematis alpina* or *C. macropetala*, the last usually with flowers that would harmonise with the gentians.

Substitutions   If you wanted to be grand, you could use the charming variegated form of the cotoneaster (in spite of its Latin specific name it grows vertically as well as horizontally). This euphorbia is the only one to use here, but is easy to obtain, starts flowering in a marvellous greeny yellow in late spring, and the flowering stems keep going until they are scarlet and green in late autumn. The lovely gentian, good in wet ground, is reasonably happy in the dry conditions provided by walls. There are many good forms of the periwinkle, from doubles in blue, burgundy and white, to fancily marked variegated sorts, but all can be invasive if they are not kept under control.

Ideas for its use   This would look good against a fence, a low retaining wall or the terraced parts of the garden. You could even use it to disguise a low outbuilding such as the log or coal shed.

1 *Cotoneaster horizontalis*
2 *Gentiana asclepiadea* (willow gentian)
3 *Euphorbia robbiae*
4 *Vinca minor* (lesser periwinkle)

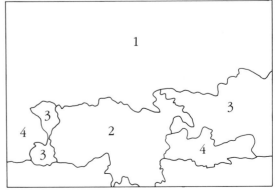

Planting 41 Architectural greenery for grand effects

For a large wall, especially if you're fond of plant architecture and restrained colours, this grand, green and generous planting could hardly be bettered. Here, on a tree in Rosemary Verey's lovely garden at Barnsley near Cirencester, it has a formal quality which would suit similar surroundings, especially a town yard. Start the planting off with ivy several years before adding the other plants.

Developments and the seasons The hellebore and daphne will give a restrained show of flowers in late spring (with gusts of perfume from the daphne in the mornings), while the wonderful leaves of all the plants are the main attraction in summer; the vine leaves turn scarlet and bronze in autumn. Everything is evergreen except the vine. It would be possible to add a third layer: perhaps *Clematis viticella* for high summer, or *C. alpina* for earlier in the season, both with glamorous blue flowers; or *C. armandii*, luxuriant and evergreen, with greenish-cream flowers and a wonderful smell of honey in February and March.

Site This planting is up a large old tree trunk, but it would do just as splendidly on a wall (preferably not too shaded), a pergola or even a shed or garage.

Maintenance and cost Maintenance is easy: only the vine is extremely vigorous and might need thinning out if it gets too big. The daphne is the only thing that might cost very much if you want a reasonably big plant.

Props and additions The planting is so lovely it hardly needs the grandiose seat – a plank bench would look almost as good, or a strapwork iron one, painted greeny blue or Indian red (not white, which would make the variegated foliage look unattractive). Some big planters beside it, perhaps terracotta pots, could be filled with soft blue agapanthus if there is room, or the annual blue- or white-flowered *Nierembergia frutescens* if not.

Substitutions In this marvellous architectural foliage combination, only the ivy could easily be changed (from what is probably a seedling from the wild), perhaps for Poet's ivy, or 'Parsley Crested'. You could try the 'Dusty Miller' grape (*Vitis vinifera*) for a more silvery effect, but nothing else would do. *Daphne retusa* would scent the area more powerfully in May, though its form is less elegant.

Ideas for its use This would suit any large expanse of wall – the planting would swamp a small fence or bungalow wall. It would look superb as a backdrop to a formal pool.

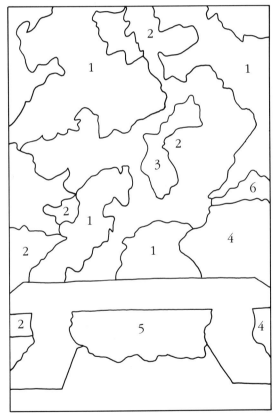

1 *Vitis coignetiae* (Japanese crimson glory vine)
2 *Euonymus fortunei* 'Variegatus' (spindle tree)
3 *Hedera helix* (common ivy)
4 *Daphne laureola*
5 *Helleborus foetidus* 'Bowles Italian Form' (stinking hellebore)
6 *Lonicera caprifolium*

Planting 42 Romantic charm for shady steps

The garden of Balbithan House, Aberdeenshire, is packed with delights (and where more are constantly planned). This planting under apple trees seems to sum up the owner's preference for old and neglected species and varieties with a few wild flowers and weeds, combined with something grand and interesting, or a plant (often a rose, pink, or auricula) saved from a ruined garden and with a name lost long ago. These lovely half-wild borders contain many familiar native species which form an excellent foil for the more exotic allium, with its rocket-like stems of beige and soft maroon flowers. Though the granite wall is part of a sixteenth- or seventeenth-century garden enclosure, the steps were built by the owner herself.

Developments and the seasons For early spring you could plant other half-wild species, such as winter aconites and some of the fancy forms of celandine (perhaps the orange-flowered one or the greenish double), tucked beside the steps, and follow these with old daffodils like 'Van Syon' and *N. eystettensis* (if you can find it; if not, use jonquils

and small varieties like 'Rip Van Winkle'). The planting as shown contains spring-flowering hellebores, which are followed in April and May by bluebells. Then this border comes into its own with the flowers seen here, and in autumn the apples overhead give ample colour.

1 *Hyacinthoides non-scriptus* (bluebell)
2 *Aquilegia* 'Hensol Harebell'
3 *Digitalis purpurea* (foxglove) mixed with *Pentaglottis sempervirens* (alkanet)
4 *Rosa spinosissima* 'Double Yellow'
5 *Helleborus orientalis* (lenten rose)
6 *Rosa*, an unnamed variety always at Balbithan
7 *Allium siculum*
8 *Lunaria annua* (honesty)
9 *Rosa* 'Alba Maxima' (Jacobite rose)
10 *Thalictrum minus*
11 *Lavandula* 'Old English' (lavender)
12 *Rosa* 'Maiden's Blush'
13 *Viola odorata* (sweet violet) mixed with *Cymbalaria muralis* (ivy-leaved toadflax)
14 Apple tree with *Rosa* 'Seagull' in its branches

ON PLAN ONLY
A *Rosa* 'Ispahan'
B *Pulmonaria* 'Pink Dawn'

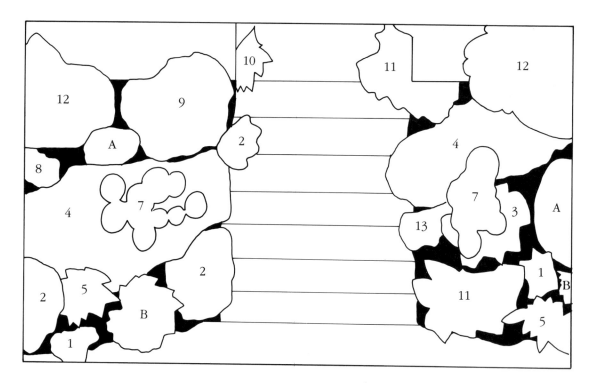

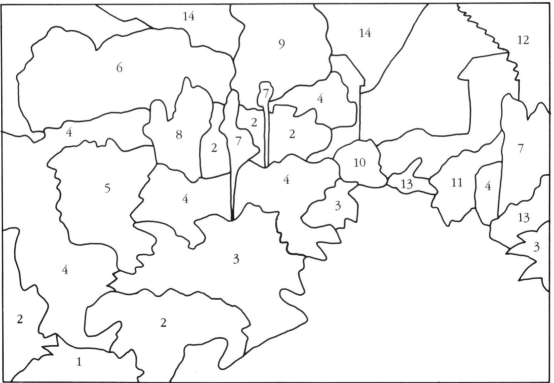

Site This planting is in the shade of some ancient apple trees, but any other lightly shaded place would suit these plants and produce the same effect.

Maintenance and cost While much of the herbaceous material here is easily grown from seed, you will need to buy in the handsome allium (more often, now, placed in the genus *Nectaroscordum*) as bulbs. Roses and apples will also need to be bought, though if you can find a friend who grows the Scots roses, ask for a few rooted runners, and you will find that these quickly make decent bushes. Maintenance is, in a border like this, a matter of taste. At Balbithan, this one gets cleared out once or twice during the spring and summer, and a major thinning every couple of years, by which time everything is almost engulfed in roses.

Props and additions Omphalodes (especially *Omphalodes cappadocica*, in the form called 'Cherry Ingram') and any pulmonarias you care to add ('Redstart' is the most marvellous brick pink, or try 'Sissinghurst White') could be added for more spring colour. On a low flag-capped wall like this, a pleasant addition would be a few low pans of echeverias or grand sedums (things you can forget to water without harm). If you have a fence, you could embellish it with standard bays or myrtles, or pyramids, in generous tubs, but nothing else.

Substitutions The wall holding the roses could easily be a low fence or slip of trellis, with the gateway marked by wooden piers, or a pair of pots or square tubs. If you don't have a suitable apple tree, plant one and wait, or even better, if you like the idea of ancient branches propped up with crutches, put in a mulberry. You will have a decent tree in ten years, though it will be more romantic-looking in a hundred. A quince or medlar, both exquisite in flower too, would be much faster. Almost any selection of rambler roses would look good here – and the granite steps could just as easily be a simple grass slope, or be made of bricks or concrete. The Scots roses are almost all lovely, in spite of a shortish season and need for regular thinning: the flowers are pretty and smell wonderful. In a small garden needing a longer season, go for the divine relative of the Scots roses, 'Stanwell Perpetual'. The blue aquilegias look good in dappled shade, but there are many other lovely sorts, from ancient doubles like 'Nora Barlow' (in soft pinks and greens), to some quite stunning whites (especially 'Munstead White'). Other alliums, too, would work nicely, especially *Allium aflatunense* or *A. rosenbachianum*.

Ideas for its use This could be used for all kinds of shady slopes, whether these are low banks or grassed steps cutting off one part of the garden from another.

Planting 43 Luxuriant sophistication for a steep bank

So many garden slopes are dull banks of ill-mown grass, or are treated as extended rockeries – with a scatter of small boulders, alpines and dwarf conifers – that it is exciting to find quite a steep slope treated with such panache that it made me long for a slope in my own garden. Here, at Walton Hall near Kelso, in the Scottish borders, the owners' artistic sense has juxtaposed interesting leaf shapes and added easy flowers, and the whole thing is set off by some good background shrubs.

Developments and the seasons For spring, rather than brash breeders' bulbs like the larger daffodils and tulips, use wildlings: lent lilies (*Narcissus pseudonarcissus*), ordinary bluebells (not, if you look at them, in the least ordinary) and sheets of dog's-tooth violets (*Erythronium* species, but especially *E. dens-canis*, which is easy from seed). From late May this planting will be in flower continuously well into early winter.

Site This is a south-facing bank leading down into a damp and shady dell, with a spring-fed pool. The bank itself is fairly dry, however, and exposed to winds blowing up the Tweed valley.

Maintenance and cost This is not an expensive planting to get into the ground, though it does need some labour input throughout the year. Weeding needs are fairly constant, and nasty things like perennial thistle, ground elder and couch grass can be taken out in autumn. The clumps of herbaceous plants look crisp here because they are well looked after; a luxuriant bank like this can easily become an impossible tangle. If you are a beginner, start off with the shrubs and let them get established for a couple of seasons while you pluck up courage to start on the herbaceous things.

Props and additions The steps and the paving used here came from a demolished building. If you can't find something similar, then concrete will have to do, though if your site is not too steep the steps could be built of logs, with the 'flats' back-filled with gravel. In this garden, there's a spring half way up the slope, which feeds a small and prettily planted pool. The top of the steps finish in a small balustraded terrace (also made of architectural fragments). Something made of rustic poles would look as good. Nothing else is needed.

Substitutions It is difficult to substitute the ligularia, though you might try *Ligularia przewalskii* (see page 27) or one of the grander rodgersias, perhaps *Rodgersia pinnata* 'Superba'. Everything else is pretty straightforward. Rather than the conifers in the background, you might prefer broad-leaved trees with bold foliage, like *Rhus typhina* 'Laciniata', or a magnolia like *Magnolia grandiflora*, or the elegant *Prunus sargentii*.

Ideas for its use This sophisticated planting would make an equally good horizontal planting, or one on a variable bank, wrapped, say, right round a pool or paved area. It would be much cheaper than stone terracing or retaining walls. If you're excavating for a pool (even a swimming pool), treat the spoil heap like this. It will look best on a straight line, not waved as a piece of cheap 'landscaping'.

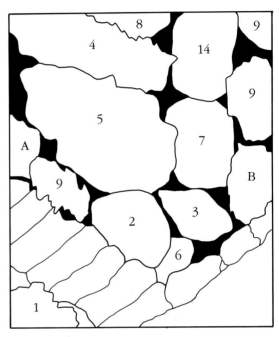

1 *Salix lanata* (woolly willow)
2 *Astilbe chinensis* 'Pumila' mixed with *A. arendsii* 'Fire'
3 *Primula florindae* (giant cowslip)
4 *Iris pseudacorus* (flag iris)
5 *Ligularia* 'Desdemona'
6 *Caltha palustris*
7 *Primula* candelabra hybrids
8 *Berberis thunbergii* 'Atropurpurea'
9 *Iris kaempferi* 'Pink Frost'
10 *Cotinus coggyria* 'Atropurpureus' (purple smoke tree)
11 *Aruncus sylvester*
12 *Achillea filipendulina* 'Gold Plate'
13 *Rosa* 'Fiona'
14 *Rosa* 'Raubritter'
15 *Tanacetum vulgare* (tansy)
16 *Cupressus* 'Sky Rocket'
17 *Cupressus leylandii*
18 *Buddleia alternifolia*

ON PLAN ONLY
A *Dryopteris filix-mas*
B *Hosta* 'Honeybells'

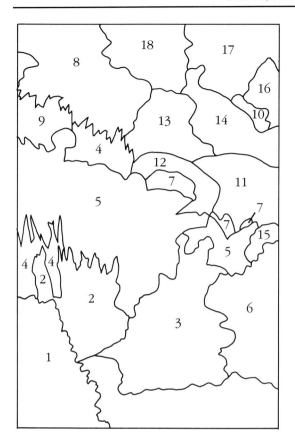

1 *Salix lanata* (woolly willow)
2 *Astilbe chinensis* 'Pumila' mixed with *A. arendsii* 'Fire'
3 *Primula florindae* (giant cowslip)
4 *Iris pseudacorus* (flag iris)
5 *Ligularia* 'Desdemona'
6 *Caltha palustris*
7. *Primula* candelabra hybrids
8 *Berberis thunbergii* 'Atropurpurea'
9 *Iris kaempferi* 'Pink Frost'
10 *Cotinus coggyria* 'Atropurpureus' (purple smoke tree)
11 *Aruncus sylvester*
12 *Achillea filipendulina* 'Gold Plate'
13 *Rosa* 'Fiona'
14 *Rosa* 'Raubritter'
15 *Tanacetum vulgare* (tansy)
16 *Cupressus* 'Sky Rocket'
17 *Cupressus leylandii*
18 *Buddleia alternifolia*

Planting 44 Climbers, knitted together, make a pretty picture

I love the effect of mixing climbers together, and this is a pleasing way of doing it, particularly because it offers a good method of softening the lurid purple of 'The President' clematis, seen here in July. It would also work with some of the other soup-plate clematis varieties (but don't try mixing different soup plates together). There are many other good things to be seen here, in the gardens of Leeds Castle in Kent; they sometimes show a bold approach to colour (though it is surprising that the building's courtyards are scarcely gardened – with all those wonderful walls reflected in the moat).

Developments and the seasons The canary creeper, which can reach a height of 4 m (12 ft) in one season, flowers for much of the time it is grow-ing, so you will have some colour early on. The clematis are in flower for at least the month of July, and sometimes during part of August. Thereafter, you might get a few curled seed heads, but little else. You could add a good foliage climber for a bit of architecture, say *Parthenocissus megalophylla* or an aristolochia. On a big wall, if you want perfume, put in the marvellously scented white-flowered *Clematis flammula*, which looks like a glamorous old-man's-beard.

Site This wall receives some shade, and its base is always shaded by lush herbaceous plantings. All these climbers will do well in full shade too, though the clematis will climb to the light and flower to the sun; your neighbour might get all the benefit.

Maintenance and cost   The tropaeolum is effectively an annual; start it off in pots early in the season, and feed once planted out. The planting will need work every late autumn, when the tropaeolum will have died off and need to be removed (save a handful of seeds), and again in early spring when you can cut the clematis plants back to about 60 cm (2 ft) above the ground, although this isn't essential. If you don't bother, the plants will still flower profusely, and rather earlier in the season too.

Props and additions   This informal and rustic planting determines the look of any props; half-barrels of flowers would do, perhaps with pink lilies mixed with night-scented stock, or a pale yellowy green kniphofia like 'Percy's Pride', or lemon yellow wallflowers, or agapanthus, or even the pot shown on page 72. If you had an arbour with this mix as a plant canopy, battered bamboo and wicker furniture would look right.

Substitutions   It would be easy to switch the deep purple clematis for something a bit paler, such as 'Lasurstern' or 'H. F. Young', but not really necessary.

Ideas for its use   This planting would work just as well on generous poles or, better still, on a pergola. It would also be suitable for trellis screens to hide an ugly view, and would make a lovely covering for some sort of arbour in which to lounge on hot summer days.

1 *Tropaeolum canariense* (canary creeper)
2 *Clematis texensis*
3 *Clematis* 'The President'
4 Apple espaliers

Planting 45 Potfuls of colour at the base of a wall shrub

This luscious planting is against a house wall at Greatham Mill, near Petersfield, Hampshire, in a garden crammed with (and selling) interesting plants. Tender plants are clustered in pots at the base of an elegant wall shrub. Pictured in early August the use of colour is particularly successful: the coral red of the fuchsia and the dusty pinks of the diascia contrast well with the yellowy green of the itea and the murky yellow of the osteospermum. The itea is at least ten years old, so you'll have to wait a while before it looks as good as this. The fuchsia is in its second or third season and is, to my mind, one of the most elegant of commercial fuchsias. (For a planting like this, avoid the overweight ballerina types.) Everything is close together, and the planting would suit a tiny garden where highly worked arrangements are needed to satisfy the eye.

Developments and the seasons The daphne will start the season in February and the pots can go out in May (they're against a house wall here, so get good protection). All will give pleasure immediately. The itea itself will be producing its flower pendants soon afterwards, and continues, with everything else, to keep going until late autumn.

Site This planting needs full sun or light shade. The itea will succeed in deeper shade; in sun it must have reasonably moist soil.

Maintenance and cost Only the handsome itea will take a bit of finding, and be particularly expensive. Most of the half-hardy plants are reasonably easy to find, and are usually cheap. Once they're all in place, maintenance is easy. Ensure that the itea stays fixed to the wall as it grows, and that the old flower spikes are removed in autumn. It's worth pinching out the growing points of the more exuberant fuchsia shoots so that the bush stays a reasonably tidy shape.

Props and additions The plants are so architectural that stone benches would look good, and so would generously scaled earthenware pots –

though lead (real or fake) tanks would look wonderful. If big enough to be filled with water, they would reflect the elegance of the plants. You need water for all those pots anyway, so a galvanised watering can would be an ideal prop.

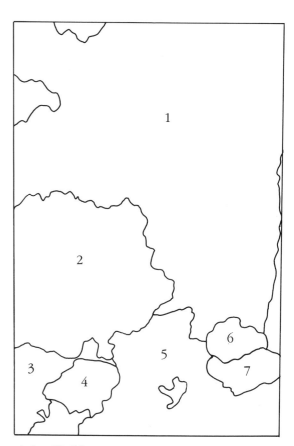

1 *Itea illicifolia*
*2 *Fuchsia* 'Thalia'
3 *Daphne odora* 'Marginata'
*4 *Helichrysum petiolatum* 'Limelight' and 'Variegata'
*5 *Osteospermum* 'Buttermilk'
6 *Diascia felthami*
7 *Lilium formosanum* 'Pricei' (lily)
   (Asterisked plants are half-hardies in pots)

Substitutions   Though there are other iteas, this is the most easily found. The lightly fragrant flowers bloom for much of the summer. You could, if you wanted winter instead of summer pendants, use *Garrya elliptica*, though the leaves are rather leaden. The osteospermum produces its marvellous soft buff-yellow flowers more freely in a small pot; with too much soil it goes for foliage instead. No other sort is quite as good, though the greenish white of 'Weetwood' might be interesting.

Ideas for its use   It would be pleasing to combine this planting with garrya on a wall, for pendant catkins in both winter and summer. Wind a yellow clematis through them, either the pretty and rather vigorous *Clematis orientalis* or the even more vigorous *C. rehderiana*, which has flowers smelling wonderfully of primroses. Wait until the shrubs are big before planting either of these. The wall would then give a fine combination of blue-greens, glossy emerald greens (the itea), soft yellows and a touch of pink.

Potager and Herb Garden

The creation of a potager is a way of gardening that recreates certain sorts of seventeenth-century kitchen gardens, where crop plants were used for their colours, textures and shapes, duplicating the kinds of effects found in the flower garden. In the seventeenth century, kitchen gardens included a much wider range of plants than they do today, for as well as comestibles and flavourings, they had to provide plants used in medicine and perfumery. Plants like lilies, lavender, artemisias, mugworts, marigolds and bloody dock were all once an important part of the kitchen garden .

Present-day potagers and herb gardens, often lovely things to look at, are also intended to produce a harvest of pretty vegetables like frilled-leaf lettuces, raddichio, fancy cabbages, red leeks and brussels sprouts, elegantly tangled as they must be amongst the roses and lavender. That means, on the whole, a lot of work to keep the spaces looking both pretty and tidy, as well as plenty of slug bait, and ingenuity. Two potagers are included here: one (for purists) makes use of no artifice, costs little and produces nothing that cannot be eaten; the other makes tasteful use of decorative plants and costs a certain amount to create, but does not give much to the kitchen.

Typical layouts for these sorts of garden are formal, and so any of the layouts of the parterres shown in this book could be used as a base plan for your edible garden. Paths should be of durable materials such as stone flags, concrete slabs or bricks (to my eye usually the prettiest). A small size of river-washed gravel could be used, but because your shoes will almost always be muddy after weeding or harvesting, the gravel tends to stick to your boots.

If you set up a formal design you'll find that it is enhanced if the paths are edged with something to strengthen the pattern, especially in winter when the crops will either be gone or half grown or looking woebegone in bad weather. Box is suitable only for a large garden, because it takes so many nutrients from the ground. Other pretty path edgings to consider include chives, runnerless alpine strawberries (grow white or yellow ones from seed), parsley, clipped hyssop and winter savory.

Once you have decided on the balance of decorative and edible plants that you want, look for interesting vegetable, soft fruit and herb varieties to grow. (Lists of seedsmen and nurseries can be found on page 155.) If you want to be able to harvest plenty of vegetables and salads, remember that the productive potager does have disadvantages: cropping will spoil the design, and you will need a constant succession of new plants coming along to fill the bare ground; you will have to keep a constant watch for pests; and the garden, unless you have a strong outline design, will look dull in winter. On the other hand, to have a potager is a good solution to the problem of what to do with the back garden if all your other needs are met. They can for much of the summer be both delightful to look at as well as productive – and if you've not tried fresh sorrel, or the young flower shoots of salsify, or asparagus peas, or proper asparagus, or your own artichokes, then you have some considerable pleasures in store.

Alternatively, you could try a garden with herbs. Because the number of herbs that can usefully be harvested for the kitchen is small, and few of them make pretty garden plants, herb gardens need either flowers or vegetables to liven them up. Most herbs are either dull to look at, invasive, or seed themselves too prolifically. Most herb gardens are motley collections of plants, many of which have no use in the kitchen, such as rue, ginger mint (a wonderful foliage plant in a big pot) and hyssop. We once planted masses of lemon balm, camomile and oswego (the lovely *Monarda didyma*), thinking that they would save on the tea bills, but we found them no substitute for a pot of Earl Grey. Even though fresh tarragon with chicken or in vinegar is wonderful every so often, tarragon invades the garden between each cropping.

The most necessary kitchen herbs are savory, thyme, purple sage (try the young shoots in spring with good cheese and wine), fennel (best in the lovely and vast purple-leafed form), apple mint, rosemary (in its white- or pink-flowered forms), chives, tarragon, a pot of basil, a row of parsley, and some chervil and dill for the very keen. The two charming herb gardens shown here are both informal, but herbs can look marvellous bounded by the formalism of a parterre (see the potagers on page 146), and this may be their most suitable habitat (if you can stop them running). Some herbs make lovely low hedges themselves, especially the shrubby thymes, almost any of the sages and lavenders, all the hyssops, winter savory, and even the tiny *Calaminta nepetoides*. All the rosemaries can be clipped, and can even be made into tall spires that you might mistake for cypresses, with a bit of help (a friend ties in drooping branches with dark green wire). Other herbs, like the gorgeous creeping Corsican mint and some of the lower-growing thymes, do well between paving stones and on low walls.

Since an extensive herb garden takes a lot of work and does not give much to the kitchen, it is best to grow your essential plants integrated into the wider garden, and have a few pots of the most used culinary things as close as you can to the kitchen door.

Planting 46 *How to make the vegetable patch come alive*

This is a potager for the purist, at Joy Larkcom's farm in Norfolk (pictured in June). Everything is edible (the stray poppy came from an earlier sowing for seed, which is one of the nicest flavourings for bread). Apart from a central metal arch for the beans, the plants are simply arranged, with paths of sand and cheap engineering brick (most 'facing' bricks are damaged by frost). The plants include a marvellous selection of interesting and unusual vegetables; Joy Larkcom is an enthusiastic collector of good things, and her salads and vegetables are among the best I have ever tasted. Her garden has plenty of room for compost and manure heaps, plastic tunnels for seedlings and experiments, so in a smaller space you might not manage such marvels, but it will still be possible to grow the most interesting vegetables you can find.

Developments and the seasons After the winter brassicas, you can harvest sorrel and chard from the end of March, and the flowering shoots of salsify and scorzonera soon afterwards (you'll be bored with broccoli and sprouts by then). The season will finish with green and golden squashes, the last beans and the first brassicas. Salads can be supplied all year if you grow such things as forcing chicories, lamb's lettuce (soon seeding itself everywhere, but delicious) and winter radishes. It helps if you have room for a frame or some cloches, though these are not easy to integrate into a pretty design.

Site This planting is slightly shaded, but fertile (there are enormous compost heaps nearby) and well watered. In an urban garden, until you have enough vegetation to make your own compost, the soil might need heavy applications of peat, bonemeal or rotted manure.

Maintenance and cost However cheap, delicious and money-saving it might be, growing vegetables, even decoratively, is not a low-labour

activity: an area of potager say 30 x 10 m (100 x 30 ft) might, if you are assiduous, take two or three days a week of your time if it is to be both pretty and highly productive. For that input, you could expect enough delicious vegetables for three or four people for the entire year (though you'd need to buy potatoes and carrots), and all the herbs, sorrel for sauces and omelettes, and flowers for the supper table that you could possibly want. You could probably have enough rhubarb, some soft fruit, and even four or five pear and apple trees.

Props and additions If this looks too rough and ready for you, add some of the elements from pages 117 and 146. In this garden, the props are plastic tunnels to grow on interesting seedlings and new crops, compost pits, hosepipes, and a loo pan planted with thyme. You might like an arbour covered with runner beans (the flowers are pretty and smell nice) over a table and some seats, where summer evenings can be enjoyed with a really fresh salad and a glass of wine. If you want some big pots, use them for mint, especially ginger mint, which can look wonderful, and won't then invade the garden. Add some night-scented stock, and a hedge of *Rosa gallica*, either the old 'Apothecary's Rose' or the striped 'Rosa Mundi'.

Substitutions The vegetables here change constantly, so it's easy to substitute as you wish. Other good things grown nearby include pansies, daisies and borage, for the colour of their flowers in salad, lovely chicories, rocket, and large numbers of oriental leaf crops (collected by the garden's owner and not all available in this country, but the seed firms on page 155 have interesting things).

Ideas for its use A small back garden could be totally given over to a potager, providing the children (if you have some) don't need anywhere to play.

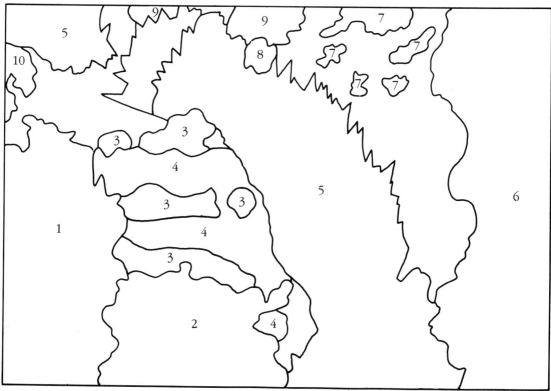

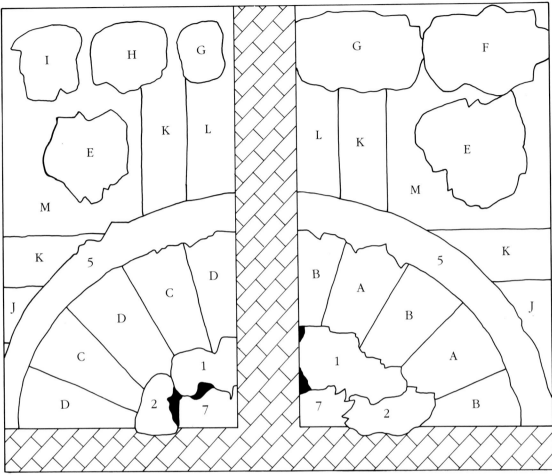

1 *Calendula officinalis* 'Neon' (marigold)
2 *Nasturtium major* 'Alaska'
3 Lettuce, bronze and green forms of 'Salad Bowl'
4 Endive seedlings, continually cropped, variety not available
5 *Allium schoenoprasum* (chives)
6 Pea 'Purple Podded' pinky purple flowers
7 French bean 'Painted Lady' pink and white flowers
8 *Papaver somniferum* 'Pink Chiffon'

9 Parsley
10 Cos lettuce

ON PLAN ONLY
A, B, C, D Lettuce and endive varieties
E Cardoon
F Artichokes
G, H, I Pea and French bean varieties
J, K, L, M Root crop varieties

Planting 47 A tunnel of vegetables and flowers

This marvellous planting on a metal framework, making a tunnel dividing one part of the kitchen garden from another, offers both visual drama and vegetables for the kitchen for much of the summer season. There's no reason why every vegetable patch should not look as exciting as this. The big leaves belong to a bright orange squash – the colour of the ripe fruit almost matches that of the rudbeckias. If you don't think that you can eat quite so many squashes (though they are delicious young, and mature ones can be stored right through the winter), try a mix of courgettes (not the 'bush' sorts, as these will not climb), some of the smaller pumpkins, and outdoor cucumbers.

Developments and the seasons Planted as here, the arbour will not be in flower until late June, and will be finished with the first frosts. It will be bare in winter, unless you plant at the tunnel ends croppable climbers like an outdoor vine (if you live in the South), or perhaps some kiwi plants (you need male and female sorts to get fruit). The vast and beautiful clary, which flowers in July, is rarely used today as a kitchen herb, though in the eighteenth century the leaves were used in fritters (nice but tough). Some marrow and squash flowers have a lovely scent, and will make the tunnel a delight to use in June; they can be stuffed, or turned into delicious fritters.

Site This planting needs an open site, and the soil must be heavily manured for all these crops.

Maintenance and cost Bear in mind that crops need 'rotating' so that pests and diseases don't build up. After two or three seasons with gourds and climbing French or runner beans, have a season or two of flowers, like morning glories, hops, or the fancy nasturtium on page 143, together with the ordinary one. (Put pigeon netting up and over the metal supports to help the plants climb.) Then you can go back to beans and marrows.

Props and additions Nothing is needed other than a rustic but comfortable seat from which to enjoy the view.

Substitutions The rudbeckias, lovely and emphatic (and sown early under glass), could be switched for marigolds, a more traditional potager crop. Try 'Art Shades' or 'Neon'. The flowers look good in salads, and were once used to add flavour and colour to stews. There are varieties of runner bean with delightful pink or pink and white flowers called 'Sunset' and 'Painted Lady'. The courgettes or squashes would look lovely if they were golden too, but some of the trailing squashes climb even more energetically than the courgettes (if short of space, try the delicious 'Jack-Be-Little').

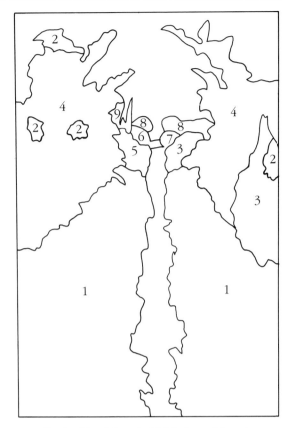

1 *Rudbeckia hirta* 'Marmalade' (black-eyed Susan)
2 *Helianthus annua* (sunflower)
3 Runner bean
4 Hubbards Golden Squash
5 *Salvia sclarea* 'Turkestanica' (clary)
6 *Oenothera biennis*
7 *Philadelphus coronarius* 'Aurea' (mock orange)
8 *Rosa* 'Little White Pet'
9 *Digitalis purpurea* (foxglove)

Ideas for its use This would make a perfect small arbour for a patio, with seats and a table, and the planting would also do well on a single-sided frame, say to screen an outbuilding or garage, the neighbours, a compost heap, or the plastic tunnels in the kitchen garden.

Planting 48 A romantic and informal herb garden

This informal and shaggy planting is in a lovely and relaxed garden in Shropshire (pictured in early June). The owner, Mirabel Osler, claims not to know much about plants (which I doubt), but she certainly knows about putting them together. The apparent artlessness of this herb garden, in which self-sown seedlings are mixed with simple plants – herbs and flowers – conceals a sophisticated eye at work. (Some of the plants, such as aquilegias and euphorbias, are poisonous.)

Developments and the seasons Early in the season, there's little in the herb garden in the way of flowering flavourings; you could provide some colour with pots of narrow scarlet tulips, or fill the central feature with hyacinths. There are double flowered ones which are very grand; better, I think, for an informal garden like this are the looser flower trusses of the 'multiflora' group.

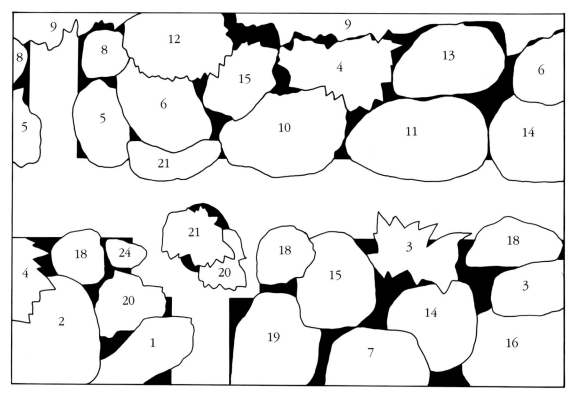

1 *Euphorbia cyparissias*	13 Bergamot
2 *Pentaglottis sempervirens* (alkanet)	14 Purple sage
3 *Papaver somniferum* (opium poppy)	15 *Aquilegia* pink spurless
4 Angelica	16 *Geum urbanum*
5 Sorrel	17 *Meconopsis cambrica* (Welsh poppy)
6 Good King Henry	18 Parsley
7 *Buddleia davidii*	19 *Mentha* 'Eau de Cologne'
8 *Iris sibirica* (Siberian iris)	20 *Alchemilla mollis* (lady's mantle)
9 *Rosa* 'Blairii No 2' and 'Bleu Magenta'	21 Common thyme
10 Tarragon	22 *Sedum* sp.
11 Tree onions	23 *Saxifraga* sp.
12 Bronze fennel	24 *Lamium maculatum* 'White Nancy'

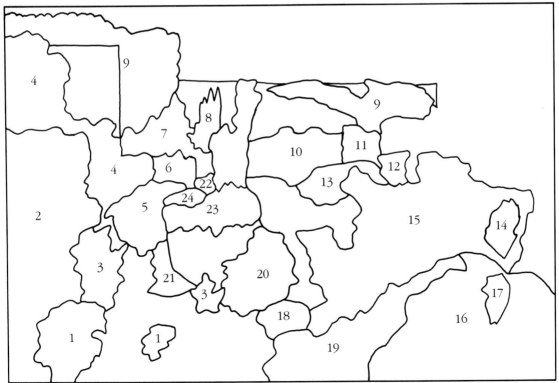

Site   This planting is in light shade but would succeed almost anywhere, including much deeper shade. The soil is good, although it is not often fed.

Maintenance and cost   None of the plants here are in the least expensive, and many of them could be grown from commercial seed (the aquilegia variety isn't sold as seed, but plants are easily obtainable). The central container, here an old copper, could as easily be a half-barrel or a bit of an oil drum as an expensive terracotta pot. The paving is roughly built from second-hand bricks. However cheap the materials, though, the maintenance will be expensive; this delectable look results from a lot of plants self-sowing, and you will need to keep weeding out unwanted things.

Props and additions   You could have more pots here, especially for the more decorative mints, apple mint and ginger mint particularly, and for white lilies and a bay tree. Among plant additions, you might like to add plenty of lavender (especially silvery pink ones), perhaps around whatever central feature you have. Sitting surrounded by it all would be a delight: seats of planking or second-hand park benches would look right, and so would a turf seat or something made with stone.

Substitutions   This enchanting herb garden is so rich in species, and has so many things self-sown, that almost everything could be substituted. Plant the plan, but you will have to wait two or three seasons before this 'look' emerges. Almost any aquilegia would do, though the pink spurless one is especially choice. It will also cross with any other you may have, and you can get some quite stunning seedlings.

Ideas for its use   So many herb gardens are dull, and only suitable for large gardens where there's a lot else to see. This one, unkempt and pretty, could easily be the only garden you have, and still not bore you. Add a few marigolds (once used to colour butter), and you can have flowers and lovely foliage from late May until the end of the season. A few vegetables, and perhaps an arch or an arbour would also make good additions. This sort of garden would also make an attractive extension to the rose parterre on page 117.

Planting 49 Roses, cabbages, lavender and leeks; formal delights

Lovely and luxuriant, this is another part of the potager shown in Planting 47. It gives visual delight as well as the occasional *bonne bouchée* for the kitchen. On a summer evening it must indeed be pleasant to wander round, sniff the lavender and the mild scent of the roses, and cut a lettuce or two.

Developments and the seasons   A few pots of bulbs would add colour in early spring, and so would a border of grape hyacinths (muscari) or tasselled hyacinths (leopoldia). The bulbs of both are used in Greek salads, and taste good. Alternatively, plant masses of cowslips, and at least pretend you will make wine from the flowers. By early summer the planting shown will be starting to look good.

Site   Most of the plants here would do in light shade, but moderately full sun would be better. The soil needs frequent feeding for the best vegetables and most abundant flowers.

Maintenance and cost The standard roses are the most expensive thing here, though making the paths can cost more than you might think. It would be cheaper, and look just as attractive, to make them from plastic woven sheeting such as Lobrene, with 3–5 cm (1–2 in) of builders' sand and the same thickness of fine gravel on top. Crazy paving sweetens the picture too much. The maintenance is as for any vegetable garden, though the final effect is a lot more fun. The box edgings need watching: their roots can drain the planting beds of nutrients, and need slicing through with a spade every second season or so. The roots that go under the path will serve the box plants well enough.

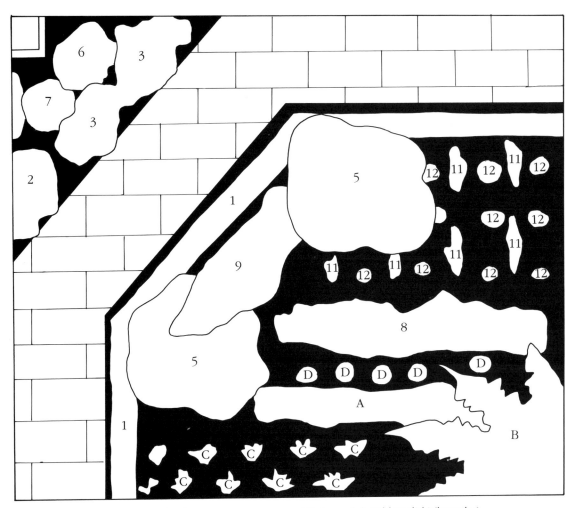

1 *Buxus sempervirens* (common box)
2 *Polyanthus* gold edged
3 Cos lettuces
4 *Lavandula* 'Hidcote' (lavender)
5 *Rosa* 'Little White Pet' (dwarf species rose)
6 Bronze lettuces run to flower
7 Decorative cabbages
8 Ruby chard
9 *Lavandula* 'Hidcote pink' (lavender)

10 *Lavandula* 'Old English' (lavender)
11 Leeks
12 Curly lettuce cultivar

ON PLAN ONLY
A Carrots
B Cardoons or rhubarb
C Sorrel interleaved with radishes
D French beans

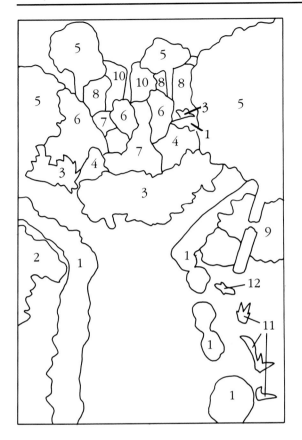

1 *Buxus sempervirens* (common box)
2 *Polyanthus* gold edged
3 Cos lettuces
4 *Lavandula* 'Hidcote' (lavender)
5 *Rosa* 'Little White Pet' (dwarf species rose)
6 Bronze lettuces run to flower
7 Decorative cabbages
8 Ruby chard
9 *Lavandula* 'Hidcote pink' (lavender)
10 *Lavandula* 'Old English' (lavender)
11 Leeks
12 Curly lettuce cultivar

Props and additions   A garden as pretty as this is practically a piece of theatre in its own right, and needs little more than a bench or two. You could have a more emphatic central feature than the urn and topiary seen here: a large tub or pot with a standard currant, or even a loquat or lemon tree would be fun; or you could have a pot as shown on page 72, or even something as theatrical as a column and pot.

Substitutions   Any number of rose varieties would look lovely here, from the usual 'Iceberg', to 'Ballerina' or some of the other hybrid musks, or even something like the luscious but sharp pink 'Comte de Chambord' (an 'old' rose which has a long season, too). If you have space, try 'Ispahan' or the wonderful 'Celeste', or even a hedge of a perpetual-flowering Scots rose like the beautiful 'Stanwell Perpetual'.

Ideas for its use   This would make a lovely back-garden planting, starting just beyond a lawn or patio, and leading (if you have enough space), through the little gate, into a tiny orchard (with medlars, quinces, filberts and bullaces) or nuttery, with the grass planted up as on page 98.

Planting 50 Flowers and herbs for a shady courtyard

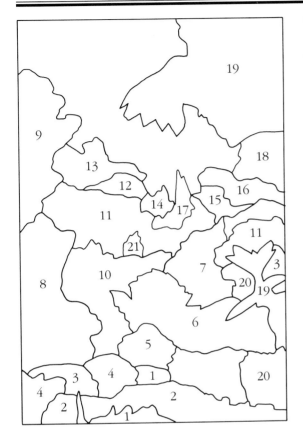

1 *Ajuga reptans* purple form
2 *Dianthus deltoides* (pink)
3 Golden thyme
4 *Erinus alpinum*
5 *Sisyrinchium angustifolium*
6 *Dryopteris filix-mas* (male fern)
7 *Allium schoenoprasum* 'Sibiricum' (giant chives)
8 *Aquilegia* 'Hensol Harebell'
9 *Valeriana pyrenaica*
10 *Poterium sanguisorba* (salad burnet)
11 *Mentha* 'Eau de Cologne' mint and others
12 *Malva moschata* white
13 *Myrrhis odorata*
14 *Sambucus niger* (elder)
15 *Allium moly*
16 *Viola cornuta* blue and white form
17 *Linaria* (toadflax)
18 *Buxus sempervirens* (common box)
19 *Rhododendron* unnamed hybrid
20 *Sisyrinchium boreale*
21 *Rosmarinus officinalis* (rosemary)

This enchanting little garden is in a partly paved and walled courtyard behind a lovely old house in Aberdeenshire. The back door is open all summer, and gusts of warm, scented air dash into the cool stone passages. Just out of view is a raised bed, crammed with auriculas and old-fashioned pinks, a perfect accompaniment to thymes and rosemary.

Developments and the seasons   This would be a perfect site for small bulbs – chionodoxas, scillas, small narcissi, species tulips and autumn-flowering crocuses. The garden as shown starts after the spring bulbs, and should give you something to smell and taste for the rest of the gardening season.

Site   This is part of a south-facing courtyard, shaded by the tall house and old fruit trees.

Maintenance and cost   Costs are low, since much is self-sown. Maintenance is mainly a matter of stopping the mint spreading, and the self-seeding things from going too far. Ruthless and regular thinning of seedlings will be important once the planting has become reasonably luxuriant. It would speed up the garden to buy as large apple trees as you can find, though these can be expensive.

Props and additions   Seats are necessary, though you might be too busy weeding during the summer to have much time to use them. In autumn you will be busy drying herbs for winter, or harvesting the fruit that falls from the tree. Pots of scented-leaf geraniums would look good. 'Rose of Bengal' and *Pelargonium tomentosum* are especially good.

Substitutions   This is another herb garden that avoids the usual dull mess of tarragon, mixed mints and unusable thymes. Substitutions are fairly easy here, and the planting could be moved more towards either herbs or flowers and still look as pretty. If your soil is limy, switch the rhododendron for something more useful, like a mulberry (which can grow quite quickly: some form fruit within a couple of seasons). If you don't have an old fruit

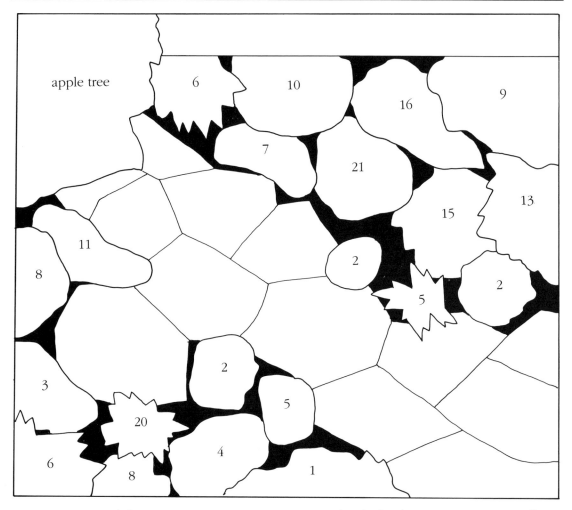

1 *Ajuga reptans* purple form
2 *Dianthus deltoides* (pink)
3 Golden thyme
4 *Erinus alpinum*
5 *Sisyrinchium angustifolium*
6 *Dryopteris filix-mas* (male fern)
7 *Allium schoenoprasum* 'Sibiricum' (giant chives)
8 *Aquilegia* 'Hensol Harebell'
9 *Valeriana pyrenaica*
10 *Poterium sanguisorba* (salad burnet)
11 *Mentha* 'Eau de Cologne' mint and others
12 *Malva moschata* white
13 *Myrrhis odorata*
14 *Sambucus niger* (elder)
15 *Allium moly*
16 *Viola cornuta* blue and white form
17 *Linaria* (toadflax)
18 *Buxus sempervirens* (common box)
19 *Rhododendron* unnamed hybrid
20 *Sisyrinchium boreale*
21 *Rosmarinus officinalis* (rosemary)

tree to give shade, plant young ones or a medlar or, almost as beautiful and rather more useful, a quince. The cracks in the paving could be filled with pinks such as 'Queen of Sheba', the gorgeous burgundy red and frilled 'Solomon' and the laced 'Sam Barlow', with 'Loveliness' allowed to seed itself around (see page 57).

Ideas for its use This would look good with a trellis margin instead of the ancient stone walls, swathed with roses, jasmine and honeysuckle. With a number of pots (try the ones on page 68), it would make a perfect backyard for a reasonably rural house.

Appendices

Appendix One: Plant Sources

The following codes are used for sources of supply:

GG suggests that a plant is generally available from garden centres;

GS suggests that a plant is generally available from major seed firms, for example Thomson and Morgan of Ipswich or Johnson's Seeds;

GH suggests that a plant is generally available from nurseries and outlets that specialise in herbs and herbal plants – though many are GS also;

GB suggests that a plant is generally available from most firms that supply bulbs for the flower garden.

Otherwise, the following codes apply. Please bear in mind that there are often other nurseries that will supply the species or variety concerned. When writing for a catalogue, either check with the business to find out if there is a charge, or at the very least include a couple of first-class stamps with your request.

Abbt   Abbot's House Garden
10 High Street
Abbot's Langley
Herts WD5 0AR
Tel: 09277 64946

Aus   David Austin
Bowling Green Lane
Albrighton
Wolverhampton
WV7 3HB
Tel: 090722 3931

Avon   Avon Bulbs
Upper Westwood
Bradford-on-Avon
Wilts BA15 8QW
Tel: 02216 3723

Bak   B. & H. M. Baker
Bourne Brook Nurseries
Greenstead Green
Halstead
Essex CO9 1RJ
Tel: 0787 472900

Beal   Peter Beale's Roses
London Road
Attleborough
Norfolk NR17 1AY
Tel: 0953 455881

Bla   Blackmore and
Langdon Ltd
Pensford
Bristol BS18 4JL
Tel: 0272 332300

Bosv   Bosvigo Plants
Bosvigo House
Bosvigo Lane
Truro
Cornwall TR1 3NH
Tel: 0872 75774

Bot   The Botanic Nursery
Rookery Nurseries
Atworth
Melksam
Wilts SN12 8NU
Tel: 0225 706597

Breg   Bregover Plants
Hillbrooke
Middlewood
Northill
Launceston
PL15 7NN
Tel: 0566 82661

Bres   Blooms of Bressingham
Diss
Norfolk IP22 2AB
Tel: 037988 464

Brid   Bridgemeer Nurseries
Bridgemeer
nr Nantwich
Cheshire CW5 7QB

Cawt   R. G. M. Cawthorne
Lower Daltons Nursery
Swanley Village
Kent BR8 7NU

Chat   Unusual Plants
Beth Chatto Gardens
Elmstead Market
Colchester
Essex CO7 7DB
Tel: 020622 2007

Clap   Clapton Court Gardens
Crewkerne
Somerset TA18 8PT
Tel: 0460 73220
0462 73220

Coto   Coton Manor Gardens
nr Guilsborough
Northampton NN6 8RQ
Tel: 0604 740219

Dix   Great Dixter Nurseries
Northiam
Rye
Sussex TN31 6PH
Tel: 07974 3107

Dra   Jack Drake
          Inshriach Alpine Nursery
          Aviemore
          Inverness PH22 1QS
          Tel: 05404 287

Eastg   Eastgrove Cottage Garden
              Nursery
          Sankyns Green, nr Shrawley
          Little Witley WR6 6LQ
          Tel: 0299 896389

Fib   Fibrex Nurseries Ltd
          Honeybourne Road
          Pebworth
          Stratford upon Avon
          CV37 8XT
          Tel: 0789 720788

Gol   Goldbrook Plants
          Hoxne, Eye
          Suffolk IP21 5AN
          Tel: 037975 770

Green   Green Farm Plants
          Bentley, Farnham
          Surrey GU10 5JX
          Tel: 0420 23202

Grov   C. W. Groves & Sons
          West Bay Road
          Bridport
          Dorset DT6 4BA
          Tel: 0308 22654

HayC   Hayward's Carnations
          The Chace Gardens
          Stakes Road, Purbrook
          Portsmouth PO7 5PL
          Tel: 0705 263047

Hil   Hillview Hardy Plants
          Worfield
          nr Bridgenorth
          Shropshire WV15 5NT

HilHo   Hill House Nursery
          Landscove, nr Ashburton
          Devon TQ13 7LY
          Tel: 080426 273

Hilli   Hilliers Nurseries
              (Winchester)
          Ampfield House
          Ampfield, nr Romsey
          SO51 9PA
          Tel: 0794 68733

Hol   Hollington Nurseries
          Woolton Hill
          Newbury
          Berks RG15 9XT
          Tel: 0635 253908

Hold   Holden Clough Nursery
          Holden, Bolton-by-Bowland
          Clitheroe
          Lancs BB7 4PF
          Tel: 02007 615

Hop   Hopleys Plants Ltd
          High Street
          Much Hadham
          Herts SG10 6BU
          Tel: 0279 842509

Ing   W. E. Ingwersen Ltd
          Birch Farm Nursery
          Gravetye, E. Grinstead
          RH19 4LE
          Tel: 0342 810236

Kaye   Reginald Kaye Ltd
          Waithman Nurseries
          Silverdale
          Carnforth
          Lancs LA5 0TY
          Tel: 0524 701252

Kel   Kelways Nurseries
          Langport
          Somerset TA10 9SL
          Tel: 0458 250521

Knap   Knaphill and Slocock
              Nurseries
          Barrs Lane
          Knaphill
          Woking, Surrey GI21 2JW
          Tel: 04867 81212

Mall   Mallorn Gardens
          Lanner Hill
          Redruth
          Cornwall TR16 6DA
          Tel: 0209 215931

Notc   Notcutts Nurseries Ltd
          Woodbridge
          Suffolk IP12 7JE
          Tel: 03943 3344

Old   Old Court Nurseries
          Colwall, nr Malvern
          Worcs WR13 6QR
          Tel: 0684 40416

OldMA   The Old Manor Nursery
          Twyning
          Glos GL13 9DU
          Tel: 0684 293516

Plea   Pleasant View Nursery
          Pleasant View
          Two Mile Oak, nr Denbury
          Newton Abbot TQ12 6DG
          Tel: 0803 813388

PP   Plants from the Past
          The Old House
          Belhaven, Dunbar
          East Lothian EH42 1NU
          Tel: 0368 63223

Prio   The Priory
          Kemerton,
          Hereford
          Open only occasionally

Ram   Ramparts Nurseries
          Hempster Farm
          Combe Martin
          N. Devon EX34 0NY
          Tel: 0276 883306

Rav   Raveningham Hall Gardens
          Norwich
          Norfolk NR14 6NS
          Tel: 050846 206

Read   Read's Nursery
          Hales Hall
          Loddon
          Norfolk

RHGR   Royal Horticultural Garden
          Rosemoor
          Great Torrington
          Devon EX38 8PH
          Tel: 0805 24067

Roo   Rookhope Nurseries
          Rookhope
          Upper Weardale
          Durham DL13 2DD
          Tel: 0388 517272

Rowd   Rowden Gardens
          Brentor
          nr Tavistock
          Devon PL19 0NG
          Tel: 0822 81275

Sav   Savill Gardens
          Crown Estate Office
          The Great Park
          Windsor
          Berks SL4 2HT
          Tel: 0753 860222

Scot   Scotts Nurseries (Merriott)
              Ltd
          Merriott
          Somerset TA16 5PL
          Tel: 0460 72306

Shre   Shrewley Gardens
          Crossways
          Shrewley
          Warwick CV35 7AU
          Tel: 092684 2402

StoHo   Stone House Cottage
        Nurseries
    Stone
    nr Kidderminster
    Worcs DY10 4BG
    Tel: 0562 69902

Stok   Stoke Lacy Herb Gardens
    Bromyard
    Hereford HR7 4JH
    Tel: 0432 820232

Thor   Thorp's Nurseries
    257 Finchhampstead Road
    Wokingham
    Berks RH11 3JT
    Tel: 0734 781181

Trea   Treasures of Tenbury Ltd
    Burford House Gardens
    Tenbury Wells
    Worcs WR15 8HQ
    Tel: 0584 810777

Wash   Washfield Nursery
    Horn's Road, Hawkhurst
    Kent TN18 4QU
    Tel: 0580 752522

Whit   Whitehouse Ivies
    Hylands Farm, Rectory Road
    Tolleshunt Knights
    Maldon
    Essex CM9 8EZ
    Tel: 0621 815782

Acanthus mollis GG
Acer palmatum 'Atropurpureum' Notc
Achillea filipendulina GG
Achillea filipendulina 'Gold Plate' GG
Achillea ptarmica 'The Pearl' GG
Achillea taygeta 'Moonshine' Bres, Dix
Aconites GB
Aconitum 'Bressingham Spire' Bres
Aconitum vulgaris 'Carneum' Roo
Actinidia kolomitka GS, GG
Adonis amurensis GB
Agapanthus campanulatus Kel
Agapanthus 'Headbourne hybrids' GS, GG
Agapanthus navy blue Rav
Ajuga reptans GG
Ajuga reptans 'Atropurpurea' GG
Alchemilla mollis seeds easy, or GG
Allium aflatunense GB
Allium christophii GB
Allium giganteum GB
Allium moly GB
Allium rosenbachianum GB
Allium schoenoprasum GH, GS
Allium siculum Avon, Rav
Alpine strawberries GS
Alstroemeria ligtu hybrids GG, GS
Anemone blanda GB
Anemone blanda 'White Splendour' GB
Anemone hupehensis GG
Anemone hupehensis 'Lady Gilmour' Hop, Kel,
Angelica GS, GH
Anise hyssop GS, PP
Anthemis cupaniana GG, PP
Anthemis 'Grallach Gold' Chat
Anthemis 'Powys Sunrise'   not in commerce
Anthemis sancta-johannis Hil
Anthemis tinctoria GS, GG
Aquilegia 'Double Pink' PP
Aquilegia 'Hensol Harebell' Trea
Aquilegia 'Munstead White' PP
Aquilegia 'Nora Barlow' GS, GG
Aquilegia 'Pink spurless' PP
Aquilegia, hybrids long-spurred GS
Aquilegia pale pink   not in commerce

Arabis albida 'Variegata' GG
Argyranthemum arguta Prio
Argyranthemum 'Jamaica Primrose' Dix, Hop, PP
Argyranthemum 'Mrs Saunders' PP
Argyranthemum 'Vancouver' PP
Aristolochia GS
Arrhenatherum bulbosum 'Variegata' Ing, PP
Artemisia ludoviciana GG, Hil
Artemisia 'Powys Castle' GG, PP
Artemisia 'Valerie Finnis' GG, PP
Aruncus sylvester GS, GG
Arundinaria anceps Hilli
Asperula azurea GS
Aspidistra Rav
Aster amellus 'King George' GG, Old
Aster macrophylla Old, PP
Aster sp. Old
Astilbe arendsii 'Fire' not in commerce. Use
   'Bressingham Beauty' – Bres
Astilbe chinensis 'Pumila' GG
Astilbe taquetii Bres, Dix
Astrantia major Kel, Old
Athyrium filix-femina GG, Fib
Aubretia GS grown, GS
Auricula 'Mrs Cairns' Blue' rarely in commerce. Use
   blue seedling GS
Avena candida (*Helictotrichon sempervirens*) GG

Ballota, Cretan form Hol
Basil 'Opal' GS
Bellis 'Alice' (and other daisies) PP, Shre
Bellium minutum Ing
Berberis thunbergii 'Atropurpurea' GG
Bergenia 'Ballawley Hybrid' GG, Dix, Hop
Bergenia 'Silberlicht' GG
Bidens ferulaefolius Hop, Rav
Blessed Thistle GS
Bronze fennel GS, GH
Bronze lettuces GS
Brunnera macrophylla 'Variegata' Hop, Trea
Buddleia alternifolia GG
Buddleia colvillei Hilli, Hop
Buddleia davidii GG

Buddleia fallowiana Hop, Sav
Buddleia globosa GG
Buxus sempervirens GG

Calendula 'Art Shades' GS
Calendula 'Neon' GS
Calendula officinalis GS
Caltha paulstris GG
Camassia leichtlinii GG
Campanula lactiflora GG
Campanula latiloba 'Alba' Bres, PP
Campanula patula Hold
Campanula persicifolia 'Telham Beauty' Hilli, Hold
Campanula porscharskyana GG, GS
Canna, purple-leaved form GB
Cardamine pratensis 'Flore Pleno' Breg, OldMA
Caryopteris clandonensis GG
Caryopteris clandonensis 'Kew Blue' Notc
Cassia corymbosa Abbt, Bot
Cedronella triphylla Hol, Hop
Celandines, double Ing
Centaurea dealbata GG
Ceratostigma willmottianum GG
Chamaecyparis obtusa 'Aurea' Hilli
Cheiranthus 'Harpur Crewe' GG, PP
Chelidonium maius 'Laciniata' Breg, PP
Choisia japonica GG
Chrysanthemum Mawii Green, OldMA
Chrysanthemum maximum GG
Chrysanthemum parthenium GS
Cichorium intybus (chicory/endive) GS
Cimicifuga racemosa GG
Cineraria maritima GS, GG
Citrus limon (Lemon) Read
Clematis 'Alba Luxurians' and other *Clematis*
    hybrids Dix, Trea, GS (species)
Cobaea scandens GS
Colchicum giganteum GB
Colchicum speciosum GB
Convolvulus mauretanica GG, PP
Cornus mas 'Elegantissima' Hilli, Rav, Sav
Corsican mint GH, PP
Corydalis cheilanthifolia Hop, PP
Corydalis lutea Abbt
Corylus avellana Hilli, Scot
Cos lettuce GS
Cosmos atrosanguinea GG
Cotinus coggyrea 'Atropurpureus' GG
Cotoneaster horizontalis GG
Courgette 'Hubbard's Golden Squash' GS
Cow parsley GS
Crambe cordifolia GG, Bres
Crocosmia 'Lady Hamilton' RHGR
Crocus sieberi GB
Crocus 'Snow Bunting' GB
Crocus susianus GB
Cupressus 'Skyrocket' GG
Curly lettuce GS

Cymbalaria muralis 'Alba' Hop, PP
Cynara cardunculus (cardoon) GS, GG

Dahlia 'Coltness' GS, GG
Daphne laureola Hilli, Scot
Daphne odora 'Marginata' GG
Datura 'Grand Marnier' Bot
Datura suaveolens GS
Decorative cabbages GS, GG
Delphiniums 'Faust' and other named hybrids
    Bla, Bres, Kel
Delphinium consolida GS
Delphinium, hybrid seedlings GS
Dianthus deltoides GS
Dianthus 'Doris' and other hybrids HayC, HilHo
Dianthus gratianopolitanus GS
Diascia felthami Green
Diascia rigescens 'Ruby field' GG
Diascia vigilis Dix, Hop
Dicentra formosa 'Alba' GG, Bres
Dicentra spectabilis GG
Digitalis ambigua GG, PP
Digitalis 'Excelsior' hybrids GS
Digitalis lutea GS, PP
Digitalis purpurea GS, Hop
Digitalis purpurea 'Alba' GS, Hop, PP
Digitalis 'Sutton's Apricot' GS, PP
Digitalis x Mertonensis GS
Dipsacus fullonum GS, Hol, Notc
Dogstooth violets GB
Dryopteris filix-mas Fib

East Lothian stocks PP
Echeveria sp. Eastg
Endive GS
Erigeron philadelphicum Breg, PP
Erinus alpinus GS
Eryngium alpinium GS, GG
Eryngium giganteum GS, GG
Eryngium maritimum GS, GG
Eryngium planum GG
Eryngium tripartitum Dix, Hop, PP
Erythronium dens-canis GB
Eucomis bicolor GB
Eucryphia x intermdia Dix, RHGR
Euonymus fortunei 'Variegata' GG
Euphorbia characias Ing, PP, Rav
Euphorbia cyparissias GG
Euphorbia martynii Hop, Rav, Trea
Euphorbia mellifera Bot, PP, Rav
Euphorbia palustris PP, Rav, RHGR
Euphorbia polychroma GG
Euphorbia robbiae GG
Euphorbia sikkimensis GG

Fatsia japonica Bot, Dix, Notc
Felicia amelloides 'Variegata' Hop, PP, Rav
Filipendula rubra Bres, Trea

Filipendula ulmaria 'Aurea' GG
Filipendula ulmaria 'Variegata' Trea, Eastg
Francoa ramosa Hop, PP
Francoa sonchifolia Hop, PP, Trea
French bean GS
French bean 'Painted Lady' GS
Fruit trees GG, Scot
Fuchsia 'Genii' and others Many widely available,
   but try Bak

Galeobdolen argentatum GG
Galtonia princeps Dix, Hop, PP
Garrya elliptica GG
Gentiana asclepiadea GG, Bot, Hop
Geranium 'Johnsons Blue' and others easily
   available GG
Geranium pratense 'Flore pleno' Bot, Kel, Trea
Geum urbanum GS, Hol
Ginger mint GH
Ginko biloba Hilli
Golden marjoram GH
Golden sage GH
Golden thyme GH
Good King Henry GS, GH
Grape hyacinths GB

Hamamelis mollis 'Pallida' GG
Hedera colchica 'Variegata' and all other ivies Whit
Helenium 'Moerheim Beauty' GG
Helianthus annua GS
Helichrysum angustifolium GG
Helichrysum microphyllum, and other species and
   varieties Ram
Heliotrope GS
Helleborus corsicus GG
Helleborus foetidus GG
Helleborus orientalis GG
Helleborus orientalis 'Black Knight' Dra
Helxine solierolii (Solierolia) Hold
Hemerocallis 'Dorothy McDade', and others Gol, Kel
Heracleum mantegazzianum GS, Rav
Hesperis matronalis GS
Heuchera 'Greenfinch' Eastg, Kel, Scot
Heuchera 'Palace Purple' GG
Heuchera sanguinea Bres, Trea
Honesty (*Lunaria annua*) GS
Honeysuckle (*Lonicera*) GG
Hostas Gol, Kel
Hyacinthoides non-scriptus GB
Hyacinths, 'Multiflora' GB
Hydrangea 'Blue Wave' GG
Hydrangea 'Bouquet Rose' Scot
Hydrangea 'Generale Comtesse de Vibraye' Bot, Hilli
Hydrangea 'Lanarth White' Dix, Scot
Hydrangea petiolaris GG
Hydrangea 'Preziosa' GG
Hydrangea serrata 'Rosalba' Hilli
Hypericum androsaemum GS

Iberis amara GS
Ilex aquifolium GG
Inula hookeri GG
Ipheion 'Wisley Blue' GB
Iresine lindenii GS
Iris 'Aline' PP
Iris 'Blue Denim' Notc, PP, Scot
Iris 'Blue Surprise' PP
Iris 'Cliffs of Dover' Coto, PP
Iris florentina GG, PP
Iris foetidissima 'Variegata' GG
Iris 'Green Spot' Bot, PP
Iris 'Harbour Blue' Aus
Iris japonica GG
Iris kaempferi GG
Iris kaempferi 'Pink Frost' Bres
Iris 'Lord Warden' PP
Iris pallida 'Variegata' GG
Iris pseudacorus GG
Iris pseudacorus 'Bastardii' Gol
Iris pseudacorus 'Variegata' GG
Iris 'Scintilla' PP
Iris sibirica GG, GS
Iris unguicularis GG, PP
Itea illicifolia GG

Jacobs ladder (see *Polemonium*)
Japanese and other maples GG
Jasminum nudiflorum GG
Jasminum officinalis GG
Jasminum stephanense GG

Kentranthus ruber GS
Kniphofia 'Atlanta' and others (for 'Lord Roberts', PP)
   Bres, Chat
Koelreuteria paniculata GG

Lady tulip (see *Tulipa clusiana*)
Lamium maculatum 'White Nancy' GG
Lavandula 'Hidcote' GG
Lavandula 'Hidcote pink' Bres, Hol, PP
Lavandula 'Old English' Eastg, PP
Lavatera trismestris GS
Leeks GS
Lemon balm (see *Melissa officinalis* 'Aurea') GG, GH
Lent Lily (see *Narcissus pseudonarcissus*)
Lettuce GS
Leucojum aestivum GB
Leucojum vernum GB
Ligularia 'Desdemona' GG
Ligularia 'Greynog Gold' Gol, Notc, Scot
Ligularia przewalskii Dix, Eastg, Hop
Lilium 'Connecticut King' and other lilies GG.
   Many species easy from GS
Linaria sp. GS
Lobelia cardinalis GS, GG
Lonicera caprifolium Hol, Hop, Scot
Lonicera japonica 'Halliana' GG

Lonicera nitida 'Baggesen's Gold' GG
Lonicera periclymenum GG
Lonicera sempervirens Hil, Hop
Lunaria annua GS
Lunaria annua (deep purple form) GS
Lunaria annua 'Variegata' GS
Lunaria annua (white) GS
Lupins GS, Kel and Brid have a good range
Lychnis chalcedonica GG, GS
Lychnis coronaria GG, GS
Lysichiton americanum Bres, Sav, Trea
Lysimachia ciliata Bres, PP, Rav
Lysimachia nummularia GG
Lysimachia punctata GG

Malus 'Royalty' Hilli, Notc
Malus 'Yellow Siberian' Hilli, Knap
Malva moschata GS
Mandragora officinalis Green, PP
Matteuccia struthiopteris Bres, Fib, Gol
Matthiola 'White perennial' PP
Meconopsis GS
Meconopsis cambrica GS
Meconopsis cambrica orange form GS
Melissa officinalis 'Aurea' GH
Mentha, 'Eau de Cologne' GH
Mentha requienii GH
Mentha rotundifolia 'Variegata' GH
Menyanthes trifoliata Rowd
Mignonette GS
Milium effusum, 'Bowles Golden' GG
Mimulus cardinalis GS, PP
Mimulus (Diplacus) cupreus Rowd
Mimulus glutinosus Hilli, Hop
Mimulus guttatus Rowd
Mimulus moschatus Eastg, PP, Rowd
Mirabilis jalapa GS
Miscanthus zebrina GG
Monarda 'Croftway Pink' GG
Monarda 'Croftway Scarlett' GG
Monarda didyma GH
Monkey puzzle tree GG
Morning glories GS
Myosotis alpestris GS
Myosotis arvensis GS
Myosotis scorpioides 'Mermaid' Dix, PP
Myrrhis odorata GS, GH

Narcissus 'Jack Snipe' and all other narcissus GB
Nasturtium major 'Alaska' GS
Nepeta 'Six Hills Giant' GG
Nicotiana affinis GS
Nicotiana langsdorfii GS
Nicotiana sylvestris GS
Nierembergia frutescens Hop
Night-scented stock
Nymphaea 'Mrs Richmond' Rowd

Oenothera biennis GS
Omphalodes cappadocica 'Cherry Ingram' Bosv, PP
Onoclea sensibilis Fib, Trea
Onopordum acanthium GS, PP
Oreganum 'Kent Beauty' OldMA
Ornithogalum nutans GB
Osmunda regalis Fib, GG
Osteospermum 'Buttermilk' GG
Osteospermum jucundum GG
Osteospermum jucundum 'Langtrees' Hop, PP
Osteospermum jucundum 'Notcutts form' Notc
Osteospermum 'Weetwood' Hop, PP

Paeonia 'Sarah Bernhardt' Aust, Bres, Hol
Paeonia lactiflora Aus
Papaver orientale GG, GS
Papaver rupifragum Eastg, PP
Papaver somniferum GS
Papaver somniferum 'Pink Chiffon' GS
Parsley (see *Petroselinum*)
Parthenocissus henryana GG
Parthenocissus megalophylla StoHo
Parthenocissus quinquefolia GG
Passiflora racemosa Hilli, Plea
Pea 'Purple-leaved' GS
Pelargonium 'Burton's Variety' and many others
    from Fib, Thor
Penstemon 'Apple Blossom' and many others from
    Gol, Green, Hop, PP
Pentaglottis sempervirens Stok
Perilla, purple-leafed GS
Perovskia atriplicifolia Bot, Hol, Rav
Persian lilacs GG
Petroselinum crispum GS
Phacelia campanularia GS
Phacelia tanacetifolia GS
Phalaris arundinacea 'Picta' GG
Pheasant's eye narcissus (see *Narcissus*)
Philadelphus 'Belle Etoile' GG
Philadelphus coronarius 'Aureus' GG
Phlox 'Border Gem' and others from Bres, Hol, Kel
Phormium tenax Gol
Polemonium foliosissimum GS
Polemonium sp. GS
Polyanthus, gold-edged GG, GS
Polygonum amplexicaule 'Inverleith' Bres, Gol
Polypodium vulgare Fib
Potentilla argyrophylla 'Atrosanguinea' GG
Potentilla nepalensis cultivar GG
Potentilla nepalensis 'Miss Willmott' Eastg, Hol, PP
Poterium sanguisorba Gol, Hol, Scot
Primula alpicola Bot, Hol, Ing
Primula, candelabra seedlings GS
Primula florindae GG
Primula veris GS, GG
Prunus laurocerasus 'Otto Lukyens' GG
Prunus sargentii Hilli, Notc, Sav

Prunus subhirtella 'Autumnalis' GG
Pulmonaria 'Cambridge Blue' and others from
    Aus, Hol, PP, Rav
Pulsatilla alpina Bot
Pulsatilla vulgaris GS, GG
Pumpkins GS
Pumpkin 'Jack-be-Little' GS
Purple sage (see *Salvia officinalis* 'Purpurascens')
Pyrethrum roseum GG
Pyrus salicifolia 'Alba' GG

Radishes GS
Ranunculus ficaria 'Anemone flowered' Ing
Rhododendron, bright pink cultivar GG
Rhododendron luteum Hilli, Trea
Rhubarb GS, GG
Rhus typhina 'Laciniata' GG
Ribes 'Brocklebankii' Gol, Knap, Notc
Rogersia aesculifolia Gol, Sav, Scot
Rogersia pinnata 'Elegans' Bres, Hol
Rogersia pinnata 'Superba' Hilli, Scot
Romneya coulteri Bot, Hilli, Hop
Rosa 'Alba Maxima' and all other roses from
    Aus, Beal
Rosemary, white-flowered OldMA, PP
Rosmarinus officinalis GG, GH
Rubus idaeus 'Aurea' Chat
Rubus ulmifolius 'Variegata' Hop
Ruby chard GS
Rudbeckia hirta GS
Rudbeckia 'Marmalade' GS
Rumex sanguineus 'Sanguineus' Bres, Hol, PP
Runner bean GS
Runner bean 'Sunset' GS

Sagina pilifera 'Aurea' Hol, Ing
Salix alba 'Argentea' Gol, Notc
Salix lanata GG
Salix 'Nancy Saunders' Mall
Salsify and scorzonera GS
Salvia grahamii Eastg, Green, RHGR
Salvia haematodes 'Indigo' Aus, Chat, Dix
Salvia nemorosa 'Superba' Bres, Dix, Kel
Salvia officinalis 'Narrow-leaved' Chat, PP, Sav
Salvia officinalis 'Purpurascens' GG, GH, PP
Salvia patens GS
Salvia patens 'Cambridge Blue' Green, PP
Salvia sclarea 'Turkestanica' GS
Sambucus niger GG
Santolina chamaecyparissus GG, GH
Scilla sibirica GB
Scilla tubergeniana GB
Scirpus tabernaemontana 'Albescens' Gol, Trea
Sedum spectabile Aus, Green, Kel
Sempervivum 'Lady Kelly' Wash
Sidalceas GS

Sidalcea 'Sussex Beauty' not traced. Try 'Rose
    Queen' Bres, Kel
Silybum marianum GS
Sisyrinchium angustifolium Chat, Ing, Trea
Sisyrinchium boreale (*S. Californicum*) GG
Skimmia japonica 'Rubella' GG
Smyrnium perfoliatum GS, GH
Solidago 'Goldenmosa' Aus, Scot, Trea
Sorrel GS, GH
Sphaeralcea munroana Green, Hop, OldMA
Spirea thunbergii Hop, Hilli, Scot
Stachys olympica GG

Tanacetum vulgare GS, GH
Tarragon GS, GH
Tasselled hyacinths (*leopoldias*) GB
Taxodium distichum GG
Taxus baccata GG
Taxus baccata 'Aurea' Hilli
Taxus baccata 'Fastigiata' GG
Thalictrum minus Aus, Bres, Ing
Thymus drucei 'Silver Posie' GG, GH
Thymus vulgaris GG, GH
Thymus x citriodorus 'Aureus' GG, GH
Thymus drucei GG, GH
Tiarella polyphylla Gol, Wash
Tovara 'Painters Palette' Eastg, Rav, Trea
Tradescantia 'Purple Dome' GG
Tree onions GH
Tropaeolum major GS
Tropaeolum peregrinum GS
Tulipa 'Peachblossom' and others GB

Valeriana pyrenaica No source found. Try
    V. officinalis Hol, Stok
Variegated hydrangea Kaye
Verbascum olympicum Chat, Rav
Verbascum phoenicicum Bres, Eastg, Scot
Verbascum 'Pink Domino' Bres, Kel, Trea
Verbena 'Hidcote purple' and others Hol, PP
Viburnum opulus 'Luteus' GG
Viburnum tinus 'Variegatum' GG
Vinca minor GG
Vinca minor 'Caerulea plena' Ing, PP, Rav
Viola 'Arkwright Ruby' Clap
Viola cornuta GG
Viola cornuta 'Lilacina' Cawt, Chat, PP
Viola 'Julian' Hol, PP
Viola odorata Grov, PP
Viola odorata 'Rosina' Grov, PP
Virginia creeper (see *Parthenocissus*)
Vitis coignetii GG
Vitis vintfera 'Dusty Miller' grape and others
    Hilli, Scot

Waldsteinia ternata GG
Wisteria sinensis, white-flowered GG

Appendix two: Gardens open to the public

These gardens are open to the public at least one or two days a year. Please note that some of the gardens illustrated are not open.

The opening times for these and other gardens to visit can be found in *Historic Houses and Castles Open to the Public* (see bibliography), in the national press, and in the regional *Gardens Scheme* booklets which appear each spring.

Planting 1 Mrs Beth Chatto's garden and nursery – unusual plants
Plantings 2 and 29 The Moortown, Shropshire
Plantings 3, 8 and 26 Plants from the Past, Belhaven, East Lothian
Planting 4 Vann, Surrey
Planting 5 Dundonnell, Ross and Cromarty
Plantings 7, 32 and 33 Stone House, Rutland
Planting 9 Stone House Cottage Nursery, Kidderminster, Hereford
Planting 10 The Priory, Kemerton, Hereford
Plantings 11, 13 and 40 Great Dixter, Sussex
Plantings 12 and 19 Crossing House, Cambridgeshire
Plantings 15 and 17 Bank House, Glenfarg, Perthshire

Plantings 16, 25 and 38 Broughton Castle, Oxfordshire
Plantings 18, 42 and 50 Balbithan House, Aberdeenshire
Planting 20 Jenkyn Place, Hampshire
Planting 21 Hidcote, Gloucestershire
Plantings 23 and 30 Powys Castle, Powys
Plantings 24 and 27 Edzell Mains, Tayside
Planting 28 The Heath, Leeds
Planting 36 Tan Cottage, N. Yorkshire
Planting 37 Levens Hall, Cumbria
Planting 39 Moseley Old Hall, Wolverhampton
Plantings 41, 47 and 49 Barnsley House, Gloucestershire
Planting 44 Leeds Castle, Kent
Planting 45 Greatham Mill, Hampshire

Bibliography

Allan, Mea, *The Tradescants: their plants, gardens, and museum*, Michael Joseph, 1964
Arber, Agnes, *Herbals, their Origin and Evolution*, 1912
Bacon, Francis, *Of Gardens: an Essay*, 1625
Berall, J. S., *The Garden: An Illustrated History*, Penguin, 1978
Blomfield, R., *The Formal Garden in England*, 1892
Bricknell, Christopher (ed.), *Gardeners' Encyclopaedia of Plants and Flowers*, Dorling Kindersley (in association with the Royal Horticultural Society), 1990
Coats, Alice M., *Garden Shrubs and their Histories*, Vista Books, 1963
Cotton, Sarah (ed.), *Guide to the Specialist Nurseries and Garden Suppliers of Britain and Ireland*, Garden Art Publishers, 1990
Harris, J., *The Artist and the Country House*, Southeby's, 1979
Historic Houses and Castles Open to the Public, British Leisure Publications, annual publication
Justice, James, *Scots Gardener's Director*, 1732
Larkcom, Joy, *The Salad Garden*, Windward, 1984
—— *Vegetables from Small Gardens*, Faber, 1989

Lloyd, Christopher, *The Adventurous Gardener*, Allen Lane, 1984
—— *The Year at Great Dixter*, Viking Penguin, 1987
Lord, Tony (ed.), *The Plant Finder* (published annually for the Hardy Plant Society)
Lovelock, Yann, *The Vegetable Book: an unnatural history*, Allen & Unwin, 1973
Parkinson, John, *Paradisi in Sole Paradisus Terrestris*, 1629
Stuart, D., *Georgian Gardens*, Robert Hale, 1979
—— *The Kitchen Garden: An Historical Guide to Tradition Crops*, Robert Hale, 1984
—— *The Garden Triumphant: A Victorian Legacy*, Viking Penguin, 1988
Stuart, D. and J. Sutherland, *Plants from the Past*, Viking Penguin, 1987
Stuart, Malcolm (ed.), *The Encyclopedia of Herbs and Herbalism*, Orbis Publishing, 1979
Thomas, Graham Stuart, *Shrub Roses of Today* (revised edition), Dent, 1980
—— *The Old Shrub Roses* (revised edition), Dent, 1980
—— *Perennial Garden Plants* (third edition), Dent, 1990

Index